Occasionally Eggs

Occasionally Eggs

Simple Vegetarian Recipes for Every Season

Alexandra Daum

appetite
by RANDOM HOUSE

Appetite by Random House® and colophon are registered trademarks of Penguin Random House LLC.

Library and Archives Canada Cataloguing in Publication is available upon request.
ISBN: 9780525611011
eBook ISBN: 9780525611028

Book design: Terri Nimmo
Cover and interior photography: Alexandra Daum
Printed and bound in China

Published in Canada by Appetite by Random House®,
a division of Penguin Random House Canada Limited.

www.penguinrandomhouse.ca

10 9 8 7 6 5 4 3 2 1

appetite
by RANDOM HOUSE | Penguin
Random House
Canada

For my mama,
who first taught me to cook, bake,
and everything else.

Contents

Introduction

When I started working on this book, the idea wasn't to make it into a seasonal recipe collection. Although using seasonal ingredients has always been an important part of my cooking style, it seemed too inaccessible, too out of touch even a few years ago—but times have changed. With our ever-changing climate, increasing concern about food systems, and growing food insecurity, it is more important than ever to try to eat seasonally. It's also easier on your wallet.

Of course, geographic location plays a large role when discussing seasonality. That is why *Occasionally Eggs* is as much about gardening as it is about cooking. I grew up in one of the world's harshest climates, on the Canadian prairies, where short and dramatic summers can reach 40°C (105°F) and long winters can hit -50°C (-60°F). Everything there grows rapidly during the hot and dry months of June to August, and sometimes into September if you're lucky—but frost can hit any month of the year. When I moved to Germany a few years ago, and then the Netherlands, I experienced true seasonal changes for the first time, and gardening here is an entirely different animal. During the winter I can grow kale, hardy herbs, cabbage, parsnips, and so on—if there's a heavy frost at all, it's often not until January. Dutch produce available in stores is often grown in greenhouses and is not as sweet and intense as the same produce grown on the Prairies. On the other hand, local produce is available year-round and I can pop into the back garden for fresh herbs and greens, even in mid-winter, which is why I include more fresh herbs in my cooking now.

I've written these recipes with my garden in mind, so most of the fruits and vegetables featured in this book are those I grow or buy at local markets and am inspired by throughout the year. I also sometimes call for bits and bobs from places far away, like pomegranate, coconut, and bananas, but only items that are easy to find in a standard grocery store in Europe or North America. Nonetheless, this is a deeply seasonal collection for anyone in the northern hemisphere. (For those in the south, please simply turn the book upside down.)

This is also a collection of recipes that reflect how my own eating and cooking have evolved. My mom's a German immigrant to Canada and we sometimes had traditional German food in the house, but she avoided it almost as much as I do—although we had a small garden and tried to grow northern European standards, like kohlrabi, that weren't locally available at the time. We sometimes ate sauerkraut and bratwurst (I hated both), or more often sweet braided breads and yeasted cakes, potato pancakes, and good dark bread, but we mostly had a lot of pasta and curry. My mom was living in Toronto when she met my dad (I was eight when we moved to Manitoba), and she embraced the Italian and Indian cooking she learned from her friends there more than the traditional German recipes she learned from her grandmother.

I learned to cook by watching my mom, then helping with little things, then cooking full meals on my own around the time I hit double digits. My mom worked a lot and my dad, if he was around to cook, could make a fried egg and not much more. I learned the typical standards first: roast chicken, mashed potatoes, rice pudding. Over time I started to incorporate what became my new standards—vegetable stews, legume burgers, and whole grain and lower-sugar desserts. Healthy vegetarian staples like these made it easier to stick to healthier eating, which is why my diet eventually became completely vegetarian.

When I started my blog, *Occasionally Eggs* (inspired largely by Angela Liddon, author of the *Oh She Glows* blog and cookbooks, gem that she is), right out of undergraduate school at twenty-one, my depression and anxiety were close to the worst they'd ever been. So in addition to being vegetarian from the start, my website features recipes with no dairy and no sugar, which makes a significant difference for me mentally. My eczema and other skin issues, bloating, and constant headaches have all largely disappeared. My crippling anxiety and daily attacks are virtually gone, and though depression has lingered, it's not to the same extent.

Nowadays, the type of food I eat and the diet I follow are largely to help manage depression, so even though I might want toast for dinner every day, it isn't the best option. That said, this book doesn't advocate a strict type of diet—it's not a health or diet book—because I believe in eating what makes you feel good instead of what other people tell you to eat. I avoid sugar and white flour because I don't like headaches, but I'll also eat a whole bag of salt and vinegar chips in one sitting. (You do you.) Although all of the recipes here are vegetarian, many work well with some animal products added in. *Occasionally Eggs* is for anyone who would like to include a veg-based meal one or more days a week, for those who are strict vegetarians, and for anyone who'd like to try to eat more seasonal food.

I've also written *Occasionally Eggs* with busy people in mind. There are plenty of on-the-go recipes: from snacks, to make-ahead meals, to quick weeknight dinners, plus basics that are great to have on hand. Some special weekend or holiday recipes are kicking around too for when you want to lose yourself in an edible project.

Throughout, simplicity is key. Just about all of the ingredients listed in these pages can be found at a regular supermarket, and I always offer alternatives or substitutions for any uncommon ingredients. Yes, many of the recipes use northern European standards like spelt, buckwheat, and some soft fruits that aren't easy to find the world over. That's because of where I live now, but I hope this book can inspire you to cook intuitively and to adapt the recipes to what's available to you regionally and seasonally and to what's in your house. Ordering online is your friend and I do a lot of it, living in a small city in a sparsely populated northeastern corner of the Netherlands. But you won't find moringa or spirulina in these pages—just a lot of lentils.

How to Use This Book

Though this book is split into the four seasons, some recipes could just as easily fit into other times of the year, and some are appropriate year-round. Look at the recipe placements here as a loose guideline you can adapt for what's in season where you live. Each season is separated into a further six sections, based on meal type or time of day.

MORNINGS AND SNACKS

Food to eat in the morning and to bring along for snacks throughout the day. Most of these are make-ahead recipes. The idea is to make a batch of something on the weekend to have through the week for breakfast or for a midday pick-me-up. There are a handful of recipes for slow mornings.

SIDES AND SMALL BITES

Side dishes, odds and ends, even a couple of very light meals. These are used throughout the book, served alongside other dishes, and are good base recipes. Think biscuits, dips, and roasted vegetables. They're great to have in the refrigerator or pantry or to make alongside a larger meal.

SOUPS AND SALADS

My favourite section of the book, with plenty of variety and an extension of mains. Most of these are full meals in themselves—all of the soups and stews are, and the majority of the salads, too. These recipes don't take long to prepare as a general rule, and make great weeknight dinners.

MAINS

A mix of quick and easy recipes for busy weekdays, and more involved ones for weekends or holidays. I think the seasonality of the book comes through most strongly in these recipes. Lots of them make great leftovers (because I'm all about a leftover lunch).

DRINKS

I haven't included a pile of smoothies, though they have their place. There are a number of warm drinks for the cooler months. While there aren't any alcoholic beverages, a couple of the drinks would make very good cocktails, and you can find recommendations within those recipes.

SWEET

Healthy-ish desserts, without any cane sugar, and a lot of fruit-sweetened recipes—plus a recipe for cinnamon rolls that I love. There are some real stunners here and a few almost instant sweets for when a sudden craving hits.

Icon Legend

Occasionally Eggs includes recipes to suit any dietary needs or preferences, and icons at the top of each recipe tell you at a glance if common allergens are left out. There's also a handy "year-round" note for recipes that are either appropriate any time of year as is or that include details on seasonal substitutions.

GLUTEN-FREE (GF) | Free from any wheat or naturally gluten-containing products. These recipes may include oats or other naturally gluten-free grains. If you are celiac, then you already know to use only certified products to avoid contamination.

NUT-FREE (NF) | Free from nuts, pretty straightforward. About a fifth of the recipes in *Occasionally Eggs* use nuts and most offer nut-free substitutions.

SUGAR-FREE (SF) | Free from any sugar that *isn't* a whole fruit. No coconut sugar, honey, or maple syrup is used. Dates might be included. Please note that recipes with this icon may include naturally occurring sugars, so some may not be suitable for a diet focused on the management of diabetes.

CONTAINS EGG (CE) | This is a vegetarian recipe but includes eggs. Since the majority of the recipes in this book are fully plant-based, this denotes those that aren't, instead of the other way around. Vegans, please avoid.

YEAR-ROUND (YR) | These recipes are suitable year-round. They either don't include season-specific ingredients or provide ideas for seasonal substitutions.

My Kitchen Essentials

If you can keep a stocked pantry and some long-lasting basics in the refrigerator or freezer, you can make a meal out of virtually nothing. Soups and stews, curries, pasta, socca—these are all easy to make with very few fresh ingredients. Beans and lentils play a big role in this book, as do garden vegetables and herbs.

I don't have a lot of space—with a small under-counter refrigerator/freezer, a very small kitchen, and little storage space—which means I don't have many extras on hand. Also, I don't freeze a lot—my freezer is the size of a shoebox—just some greens, frozen peas, and basics. When I've had more freezer space, I've always kept a series of cooked legumes, maybe a loaf of sourdough, fruit and veg, stock, and a variety of soups that freeze well. Opportunities and instructions on freezing these items are all noted in the recipes if you like to stock up.

Every recipe notes storage time, either refrigerated, frozen, or at room temperature. I've written those guidelines with North American readers in mind, because although I grew up keeping leftovers on the counter (which I still do), I know it's not so common when you have a big refrigerator! My husband still thinks it's strange to keep food out overnight.

You won't find any superfood powders or trendy bits and bobs in my kitchen or pantry. The only real exception to this is chia, which is relatively cheap, is a good binder in vegan baking, and doesn't taste like anything. I like to keep things simple (and affordable), and even though I eat mostly plant-based, it's a whole food, real food approach, rather than something based on a colourful powder that tastes like dishwater.

These are the essentials I have on hand at almost all times. They're not the only items used in the book—you'll read more about ingredients used in my recipes later in this section—but can be a good starting point. If some of the ingredients sound foreign, don't worry, explanations and substitutions are outlined in the Common Ingredients section (page 13).

FREEZER
- Soaked red lentils and other soaked lentils
- Cooked beans and chickpeas (see page 11)
- Frozen spinach and peas
- Vegetable Stock (page 243)
- Frozen berries

REFRIGERATOR

· Non-dairy milk

· Coconut yogurt

· Eggs

· Mustard

· Ginger

· Maple syrup

· Cabbage, carrots, apples—things that last a long time at the back of the refrigerator

· Sauerkraut

PANTRY

· Extra virgin olive oil

· Coconut oil

· Grapeseed oil, hazelnut oil, walnut oil, other nut oils

· Seeds: chia, pumpkin, sunflower

· Grains: brown rice, bulgur, oats, quinoa

· Pasta (I like spelt, but kamut, legume, and whole wheat pastas are all great)

· Flours: spelt (light and whole grain), rye, buckwheat

· Arrowroot powder

· Cocoa powder (and/or raw cacao)

· Coconut sugar

· Honey

· Dried pulses: beans, chickpeas, lentils

· Canned tomatoes

· Canned beans

· Dried fruits: dates, raisins, unsweetened shredded coconut

· Fruit bowl: bananas, lemons, and whatever's in season

· Spices: bay leaves, cardamom, cayenne pepper, cinnamon, coriander, cumin, fenugreek, herbes de Provence, sea salt, sumac, turmeric

EQUIPMENT

I have an absolutely tiny kitchen, with literally no cupboard space—it's about 8 feet (2.5 metres) wide, one wall, that's it—so I don't have a lot of equipment. I used to have a good blender, standing mixer, and electric mixer—all the upscale kitchen stuff—but when I moved overseas, I sold all of it and then started here without anything. You'd be surprised, even for someone who works full time creating recipes, how little of this stuff you need. I knead bread by hand, whip cream and make meringue with a whisk, and use an immersion blender for blending. I don't even have a chef's knife. Every recipe in this book can be made with very basic equipment.

Food Processor: I use about the cheapest one you can get, and it's what I used during the whole testing process for this book. No need to get a crazy expensive one!

Pepper Mill: I went a few months without one recently, and pre-ground pepper tastes like dirt. Again, doesn't need to be fancy, just needs to grind.

Hand Mixer or Blender: I didn't use a blender once in the writing or recipe testing of this book. I have a decent immersion blender (sometimes called a stick or hand blender) and use that to make things like milk, smoothies, and puréed soups. A high-powered hand blender costs maybe forty dollars and can do anything a regular blender can do—and it takes up much less space. So no, I don't have a Vitamix. For a good hand mixer, look for one with 800-plus watts; this is enough power to make any of the blended recipes in this book.

Dutch Oven: I have a nice cast-iron one from Skeppshult that (full disclosure) they sent me for free. The lid doubles as a frying pan, and it's the only frying pan I own. It's the best and most-used kitchen item I own, without a doubt.

A Few Pots: They don't need to be great ones, but they should have lids. No recipe in this book needs more than a standard large pot, because that's the biggest one I have.

A Few More Things:

- Wooden spoons
- Big whisk
- Paring knives
- Cooling rack
- 8-inch (20 cm) springform pan
- Standard bread tin (9¼ inches / 23.5 cm long)

How to Cook Grains and Legumes

All of these guidelines are based on having soaked the grain or legume overnight, which reduces cooking time and can make it easier to digest. To be sure your beans are cooked, cut one in half; if it still has a light, hard node in the centre, it needs more time. Using baking soda in the soaking water for beans and chickpeas reduces the cooking time, and using it in the cooking water results in very soft legumes.

For all of the legumes, there are a few things to keep in mind. First, all the water shouldn't be absorbed when cooking them. If too much water evaporates during cooking, simply add more to cover. Rinse very well after cooking and before eating or storing. For storage, they can be refrigerated in a sealed container for about a week and frozen for up to 3 months. I usually freeze them in jars with some space at the top for expansion. Beans and chickpeas should not be cooked with salt—it increases the cooking time—but lentils can be. Adding a piece of kombu seaweed while cooking legumes can help to reduce the gaseous effects, as does soaking overnight.

If you're not 100 percent confident in the quality of the grains or legumes you're using, pour them out onto a rimmed baking sheet beforehand to quickly see if any stones need to be picked out. Rinse any dust off in a fine-mesh sieve if they're not clean.

GRAINS AND LEGUMES	COOKING METHOD
Short Grain Brown Rice	Soak the rice for at least 12 hours ahead of time. Add 1 part rice to 1½ parts well salted water and bring to a boil over high heat, then reduce the heat to low and simmer, covered, for 15 to 20 minutes. If you want to freeze the rice, it's best to freeze it soaked (and drained) but uncooked. When thawed, it needs a shorter cooking time and doesn't get glue-like. I freeze it in portions in glass jars, simply rinsing well and draining any excess water before freezing.
Quinoa	Soak the quinoa for at least 12 hours ahead of time. Add 1 part quinoa to 1½ parts well salted water and bring to a boil over high heat. Reduce to medium-low and simmer, covered, for 10 to 15 minutes. Quinoa can be frozen in the same way as brown rice (noted above).
Chickpeas	Soak the dried chickpeas overnight, with a sprinkle of baking soda, and rinse well before cooking. For firmer chickpeas, to use in falafel or salads, generously cover with water and bring to a boil over high heat. Reduce the temperature to medium-low and simmer, covered, for about 2 hours. For very soft chickpeas, best for hummus, cook the same way, just adding another sprinkle of baking soda to the water before cooking.
White Beans	For both large and small dried white beans, soak the beans overnight with a sprinkle of baking soda. Rinse well, then add the beans to a large pot and cover generously with water. Bring to a boil over high heat, then reduce to medium-low and cook, covered, for about 2 hours, or until cooked through.
Black Beans	Soak the dried black beans for 24 hours with a sprinkle of baking soda. Rinse well and place in a large pot. Cover generously with water and bring to a boil over high heat, then reduce to medium-low and simmer, covered, for about 1½ hours, until soft.
Kidney Beans	Soak the dried kidney beans overnight with a sprinkle of baking soda. Rinse well before adding to a large pot and covering with water. Bring to a boil over high heat, then reduce to medium-low and cook, covered, for about 1½ hours, until soft.
Red Lentils	Red lentils are more delicate than other types of lentils and shouldn't be cooked separately from the dish they will be added to. When cooked alone, they break down almost completely. I like to soak a full package overnight, then freeze in jars large enough for a pot of soup or the Harissa No-Meat Balls (page 192). They need a short time to thaw in hot water and cook very quickly. They don't need to be soaked, but it reduces the cooking time and I like to have them on hand for making patties.
Brown (Mountain) and Puy (French Green) Lentils	Soak the dried lentils overnight. Rinse well, then add to a medium pot and cover generously with salted water. Bring to a boil over high heat, then reduce to medium-low and simmer, covered, for 35 to 45 minutes. The lentils should retain some texture when cooked.
Black (Beluga) Lentils	Soak the dried lentils overnight. Rinse, then add to a medium pot and cover generously with salted water. Bring to a boil over high heat, then reduce to medium-low and cook, covered, for about 20 minutes.

Common Ingredients

I've walked a fine line in this book, trying to write recipes that are accessible without being boring. So I've used ingredients that aren't too foreign, although some niche items pop up every now and then. With that in mind, there aren't a pile of alternative flours or really crazy spices—even sumac and smoked paprika can be easily found these days. If recipes are gluten-free, for example, I've tried to keep the number of flour types to a minimum. You're not going to find Himalayan pink salt as the recommended seasoning here, but there are recipes using delicata squash. Substitutions are provided for any harder-to-find products; I get how frustrating it is to see a cookbook and know that you can't get any of the ingredients.

Much of this book is based on seasonal food, whether that's grown yourself or bought at a market or in a grocery store. I often hear from people who are part of CSAs (community supported agriculture programs) that they sometimes don't know what to do with the produce they receive each week, and I hope that this book might help.

My husband and I moved into a new house shortly before I started working on this book, with a back garden completely paved with bricks and a front and side garden filled with plastic sheeting and rocks. We ripped it all up and filled it with vegetables and insect-friendly flowers instead, so I created recipes with what I was growing. That's why you see a lot of herbs throughout. Fresh herbs are pricey, so if you're not growing them, you can often substitute dried in their place. I skipped over recipes using piles of fresh herbs when I was really struggling financially, and used a lot of herbes de Provence, dried dill, and aromatic spices instead.

I grew up cooking without recipes, watching my mom cook from memory or create something new when she was in the kitchen, and I follow the same rules. Though I write recipes for a living, I see them, to some extent, as flexible creatures. Using coconut flour instead of all-purpose, no. Switching sumac for lemon zest, yes. Something I encourage you to do with this book, and in general, is to experiment with tastes and ingredients you prefer. If you like a lot of acid, increase the lemon (or the opposite). Use the type of pumpkin you have on hand. Season to your taste. Intuitive cooking is important, whether you follow recipes exactly in your kitchen or not.

With that in mind, here are the ingredients I use most often in my kitchen and those found throughout this book.

VEGETABLES

Greens: In cooking, "hardy greens" refer to those that can handle a bit of heat—spinach, arugula (rucola), chard, kale, beet and celery greens, and so on. These are mostly interchangeable; you don't want to sub kale for spinach in a salad without some work beforehand (i.e., giving it a quick massage), but spinach can be used in place of kale in a soup. Kale and chard can always be substituted for one another. You'll want to remove the woody stems from these.

Salad greens depend on the use. Leaf lettuce won't hold up to anything warm without melting, essentially, but Little Gem doesn't mind as much.

My personal favourite, across the board, is arugula. It's excellent in everything from salad to stews, with a light peppery flavour and no hard stem.

Onions: When a recipe calls for a medium onion, it's about the size of a tennis ball, not the head-sized onions found in supermarkets across North America. Small is about half that size, and a large onion is about the size of a fist. Onions are absolutely minuscule in Europe for some reason and peeling is a nightmare, I tell you.

Root Vegetables: Generally unpeeled unless absolutely necessary. The peel is where most of the antioxidants are, did you know? Also, I hate peeling vegetables, as I imagine most people do, and carrots really don't need it (but beets do). Just give them a good scrub unless you're very uncertain of what may be lurking on the skin.

Brassicas: These include cauliflower, broccoli, cabbages, kohlrabi, and so much more.

Brassicas can be pricier because they are so difficult to grow, but they are a real seasonal treasure. They are used fairly extensively in this book—though I tried to keep the very northern European recipes to a minimum—and can often be found organic, even in regions with the lowest accessibility. If yours are looking a bit brown on top, use a small grater to remove those bits before cooking.

Summer Vegetables: Summer, or soft, vegetables include tomatoes, zucchinis, eggplants (aubergines), and peppers. Zucchinis and eggplants should be eaten when still rather small, so if you're at the market and the price is per piece, don't go with the urge to get the largest one. It's not good for anything but shredding and hiding in something. When listed in a recipe, medium means about the length of an average adult hand for zucchini and eggplant. Tomatoes are the size of a standard round or plum tomato, though a weight is generally given, and peppers are the standard four-chamber red bell pepper.

FRUITS

Citrus: "Juice of 1 lemon" is frequently used in the ingredient lists, and it's about 2 to 3 tablespoons. If you have giant lemons, use your discretion and just use half. If they're tiny, you might need two. Like salt, this must be done to personal preference, as you might like a less acidic dish. Juice of a lime is about 2 tablespoons.

Lemon zest is another frequent player in my recipes. Unwaxed organic lemons are going to be best here. Grate them on a handheld zester or zesting side of a box grater, but don't go down to the white, or pith, as it's bitter. Same goes for orange zest.

Oranges can be any variety you like. I like Valencia and other sweet oranges, but generally, any variety available when they're in season will be good.

Common Fruits: Apples are good just about year-round because they store so well, though they're in season in autumn. If the only apples for sale in spring are imported from across the ocean, ignore them—they are not worth your time. My apple choices generally include Braeburn, Cox's Orange Pippin, Elstar, Jonathan, and Belle de Boskoop. I avoid Granny Smith and Red Delicious if buying from the grocery store, as they often lack both flavour and texture. As with anything, look for local, and only

use apples you like on their own in cooking and baking. There's just one pear recipe in this book, but pears can often be substituted for apples.

Bananas should be very ripe when used for any of the recipes in this book because they're usually contributing to the sweetness, and so should be at least slightly past the pure yellow stage and starting to spot.

Soft Fruits: I categorize berries, figs, grapes, and persimmons as soft fruits. They should be free from bruises and as fresh as you can get them because they lose flavour and start to break down almost instantly after being picked. They are largely useless and taste like water out of season.

Stone Fruits: Stone fruits are really only in season in summer and early autumn, and they are gems while they last. Plums, apricots, nectarines, peaches—precious. Apricots are available in late spring, and plums go right up into autumn. Again, they are best fresh. Stone fruits should be slightly soft to the touch and don't last long once ripe.

Frozen Fruits: Berries in particular should be a freezer staple for smoothies, crumbles, and more. Frozen mangoes and peaches are usually good to buy, and overripe bananas can be frozen either whole (peeled) or in chunks for drinks and fruit-based ice cream, like the strawberry version on page 60. Frozen bananas add creaminess to smoothies and can even be thawed for baking.

FLOURS AND GRAINS

In North America, you can find any of the less common grains and pulses at Flourist, an incredible Canadian company based in Vancouver, or through Bob's Red Mill.

Spelt: This is the flour used most often in the book. Spelt flour is most like regular wheat flour but can be a bit easier on the stomach. It's a bit nutty, with a pleasant taste, and is very easy to work with. Spelt is becoming more and more available, but if you can't find it, regular flour can be used 1:1 instead.

In most dessert or pastry recipes, I choose light spelt. That being said, it can be tricky to find and can often be substituted with whole grain spelt or whole wheat pastry flour with good results. My friend Kelly tested the Lemon Vanilla Layer Cake (page 64) with whole grain spelt flour, and she and her family, including a very opinionated toddler, loved it.

If the type of spelt is not specified, you can use light, whole grain, or a mix of the two at your discretion. If light spelt is specified for a recipe, like in a pastry, it's because the dish will become heavy if whole grain spelt flour is used. I generally choose fibre-rich whole spelt, but if you're new to it, it's worth doing a mix to begin with. Light spelt is more like all-purpose flour, and whole spelt is like whole wheat flour.

Oat: In this book, oat flour is considered gluten-free, because oats are, and if it's really important that they're completely free of trace wheat, you can easily find that nowadays. Oats are cheap as dirt and make a great flour for both sweet and savoury baking, so you'll see it used quite a lot throughout the book. If a recipe calls for oat flour, make sure it's finely ground.

Buckwheat: Also cheap but generally heavier than oat flour, buckwheat has a nice deep flavour. I grew up with buckwheat flour, especially for German pancakes, and I like the taste. It's not for everyone, though, and the texture is a little different—denser but very fine, as buckwheat flour is made from a seed. When buckwheat flour is listed in a recipe in this book, it's always whole grain, but light buckwheat will work as well.

Chickpea: Excellent for binding and savoury baking, chickpea flour is a workhorse. It's not so good in sweet baking unless masked with chocolate or another strong taste, but it's a solid egg substitute in many cases and good in recipes that don't need to rise much. Chickpea flour tastes and smells disgusting when raw, so don't taste (and avoid smelling) it while prepping, as you will be unpleasantly surprised.

Alternative Flours: Kamut, einkorn, Red Fife, red spring, and any ancient wheat variety can be subbed for spelt in these recipes. If there are simple ways to make a recipe gluten-free without using a number of different flours and starches, those recipes are marked "GF." A good all-purpose gluten-free flour can be substituted for most recipes calling for spelt flour if you can't eat gluten, like the blend from Bob's Red Mill. I have not included gluten-free substitutions for each recipe because I haven't tested them all with gluten-free flour, so I can't guarantee that they'll all turn out perfectly. I beg of you, don't use coconut flour.

Rice: Short grain brown rice is my go-to, but I haven't specified types of rice in any recipes because it's always cooked separately from other elements, so you don't need to worry about different cooking times. I choose brown rice for the higher fibre content (though white rice is pretty great), but use any kind of rice you like.

Freekeh: Freekeh is featured just once in this book. It's a roasted cracked wheat and has a pleasant toothsome texture and nutty flavour. If you can't find it, quinoa or rice can be substituted in its place.

Quinoa: Just a few recipes here use quinoa, but it can be a great element in dishes and makes a good side. Quinoa sometimes needs to be rinsed before cooking, but many brands now come pre-rinsed. Check the label to make sure; quinoa is coated in saponins, which can make it very bitter if not rinsed off.

BEANS AND LEGUMES

Lentils: I like cooking with red lentils, French green (Puy) lentils, brown (mountain) lentils, and black (beluga) lentils. They're cheap, easy to prepare, and taste great. I often soak lentils ahead of time, if possible, to reduce the cooking time and make them a bit easier on the stomach. Lentils called for in recipes throughout this book are uncooked unless specified.

Beans and Chickpeas: I use a variety of beans throughout this book, including small and large white beans, black beans, and kidney beans, as well as chickpeas. My recipes always call for cooked or canned unless otherwise noted. When buying canned, look for brands without any added ingredients—it should just be the type of bean and water (no salt or anything else). If I'm using canned, I like to rinse them once, then give them a soak in fresh water for as long as I can while prepping other ingredients, and then rinse again. I might be imagining it, but I think they taste better this way, and it seems to reduce the gaseous effects.

FATS

Olive Oil: Olive oil is ideal for cooking and baking, and I don't buy into the constantly conflicting information about whether it's good for cooking or not. The best choice for vinaigrettes and dressings, olive oil is also good for sweets, and I use it more than any other ingredient in the kitchen by far. I always choose extra virgin for both cooking and raw uses.

Coconut Oil: Coconut oil is always used solid, at room temperature, unless otherwise noted. It's not used extensively in this book, but it is a good non-dairy fat for bakes that need a bit more structure after cooling, because it does solidify. I use unrefined coconut oil, as I don't mind if there's a very slight coconut flavour, but if you don't like it, go with refined instead.

Nut and Seed Butters: A true saviour in plant-based food is a good nut or seed butter. It adds depth and richness much like eggs and butter do, and helps to add structure when needed. A vegan cookie is simply not good without it. It does, however, alter the taste of whatever you're making to a large degree, so use what you like. If you find tahini too bitter, then choose a different option, like peanut or almond. I generally go for homemade (page 240) or plain old (natural) peanut butter.

SEASONINGS

Acid: A touch of acidity, often lemon juice or apple cider vinegar, will bring the recipes in this cookbook to life. This is especially true for soups and stews, which can often fall into a pit of blandness. If you taste a soup and find it flat, add a splash of lemon or vinegar (apple, wine, or balsamic) before reaching for the salt.

Salt: I use fine-grained sea salt when I cook. I tend to use a rather heavy hand with salt, but I've kept added salt fairly minimal here, so that is not to my taste—rather, yours. Many of my testers noted that they halved the salt used in the first round of testing, which may be due partly to differences in salt by region. Be sure to taste and add seasoning as needed, particularly with broth-based dishes. If you think you're bad at making soup, you probably just need to add salt.

Pepper: Pepper is always freshly ground, and either black or mixed peppercorns. Pre-ground pepper is terrible and never worth the money. A couple of recipes call for pink pepper—if you can't find it, either leave it out or use black.

SPICES

A number of spices are used throughout this cookbook, but the most common ones in my pantry are cinnamon, nutmeg, cardamom, cumin, cayenne pepper, and turmeric. If you don't want to go crazy with buying spices, these will have you covered. In fact, these spices made up my full spice cupboard for years when I was broke. Now that cupboard has expanded to include things like sumac, bay leaves, fenugreek, coriander, saffron, mustard seeds, paprika, and more.

HERBS

Fresh herbs are used extensively throughout my recipes. They are always fresh unless otherwise noted. I know herbs are expensive if you don't grow them yourself, and substitutions are often provided with that in mind. Leaves should be removed from stems, especially with varieties like thyme and basil, unless noted.

I don't use dried herbs often, only occasionally, and generally only herbes de Provence. Try to find a blend without lavender, or with lavender near the end of the ingredient list. Basil is utterly useless dried, so I don't recommend buying it, but dried oregano and thyme are useful to have on hand. Freeze-dried herbs are also good, with a better flavour and colour than store-bought jarred dried herbs.

SWEETENERS

No cane sugar is used in this book apart from in a couple of the fermented recipes. I don't really think that the types of sweeteners I use are healthier than regular sugar, but they do add an extra element to the dishes and another layer of flavour, which is often needed in dairy-free baking. Plain sugar is boring.

Honey: This is my sweetener of choice now because it's local and relatively inexpensive. Honey is still sugar, so I'm not using cups and cups of the stuff, and it can deeply alter the flavour of a dish depending on the type you use. I usually go for summer blossom honey, even though I will always have a special place

in my heart for canola honey. Runny or creamed, it doesn't matter, unless specified. I don't specify whether to use raw honey or not. You can choose to use raw in recipes that aren't heated, but don't use it in baking or cooking, as you'll lose any possible benefits.

Maple Syrup: Maple syrup is great. You can use maple syrup in place of honey for any recipe in this book to make it fully vegan. I don't use it that much where I live now because it's all imported from Canada and so expensive, but I go nuts when I'm home, and personally prefer it to honey for most things. It is slightly less sweet than honey.

Coconut Sugar: Coconut sugar is a bit drier than white sugar and can't really be used 1:1 despite what the companies that sell it want you to believe; you generally have to add more liquid to a recipe when you use coconut sugar. It has a very pleasant caramel flavour and it's what I choose for recipes like cookies or those that don't do as well with a liquid sweetener. Despite its similarity to cane sugar and ease of use in baking, it's not my first choice, as it's imported from such a great distance.

Dates and Other Fruits: I use Deglet Noor dates, which come in large packages and are usually pitted. They're much less expensive than Medjool dates and work just as well. In recipes that call for soft dates, either use fresher dates with a softer texture or soak them in very hot water for 30 minutes before draining and using.

Using fruit as a sweetener is great for a couple of reasons: their added fibre makes it easier to metabolize the sugars, they often help to hold baking together, and they add flavour. Recipes that use only fruit as a sweetener are considered sugar-free in this book. You'll see dates used several times, and other times banana and apple.

Vanilla: Part of the reason vanilla is used in virtually every bake ever is because a little goes a long way, both for flavouring and for sweetness. Like cinnamon, it makes things taste sweeter without extra sugar. I make my own extract because it's so hard to find in Europe: just a few beans in a bottle of brandy or vodka. Or I'll use powder or paste if I'm lucky enough to get it as a gift. Vanilla powder is my top choice, but it's gotten way too expensive in the past few years, and extract is more cost-effective and easier to use. Whenever a recipe calls for vanilla, it's extract. To sub in powder or paste, reduce the quantity by half.

EVERYTHING ELSE

Non-Dairy Milk: A handful of recipes are provided near the end of this book for making your own milk (page 237). I primarily use homemade oat milk but go for cashew if I'm feeling fancy, or hemp. Any nut-based or other light milk (not canned coconut) can be used for any of the recipes that call simply for non-dairy milk. Full-fat coconut milk is specified in some recipes. Dairy milk can be used any time non-dairy milk is called for if you include dairy in your diet.

Yogurt: A recipe for coconut yogurt is included in the Fermented chapter (page 213), but I often buy coconut yogurt as well. I look for a very short ingredient list and try to find an unsweetened version. Ideally it should just be coconut milk, cultures, and some sort of starch as a thickener. I sometimes buy

cashew, almond, and oat yogurt, but not very often.

Cocoa and Raw Cacao Powder: Cocoa powder is called for in recipes that are baked or cooked in some way. I use natural cocoa, not Dutch process. Usually if the brand you're purchasing doesn't specify that it's Dutch process, then it's natural and fine to use here. Make sure you're getting pure cocoa powder and not a mix with added sugar.

Raw cacao is stronger and used more sparingly. Raw is used only in recipes that aren't baked in this book, as there are supposed to be some extra health benefits associated with it (and because it's much more expensive). Cocoa powder can be used in place of raw cacao, but not the other way around.

Spring

With spring comes the true beginning of the year, in the form of new life in the garden and on our plates. The first fresh ingredients arrive after the hungry gap of late winter and very early spring, first with wild garlic and nettle to forage, then early crops in the garden.

I struggle in winter, as most people with depression do, and spring lifts a weight that, over the previous few months, has become so familiar that it is easily forgotten. With lengthening days and more light, spring is special in more ways than new produce. More time outdoors lifts the spirits. Fresh greens bring colour to a drab end-of-season palette. Berries arrive, along with radishes, asparagus, and new potatoes.

Spring may be my favourite season—though not in Manitoba, where it's more of a mud season before the heat suddenly hits. There is such a feeling of new beginnings, and although we associate summer (more late summer and autumn) with an overabundance and harvest time, spring is much the same. It's a busy time of year.

You'll see plenty of asparagus and other greens throughout this chapter. I've tried to keep early and late spring as separate as possible, and haven't included any ingredients like ramps that need to be foraged (though the spring green soup would be excellent with ramp pesto). At this time of year, adding asparagus and any other available greens to pizza is one of my favourite ways to eat them.

Strawberries, likely the most quintessential spring produce, make several appearances. You may be surprised by some of the strawberry pairings offered here, from coriander in a spiced jam to pickled beets and crackers served alongside on a platter. There are the more classic lemon and chocolate pairings, too, of course. When strawberries are at their best, I often eat all of them before they can make it into a finished dish, but they are spectacular combined with such a breadth of ingredients.

There is a particular freshness to spring, and I hope that comes through in this chapter. A mix of comfort food and cooling recipes for the rare hot days of this season, some excellent picnic recipes, and lots of herbs. And a potato salad, of course, because potatoes are the best food no matter the time of year.

GF | YR

When I was a kid, we rotated going to Germany and my Omi coming to visit us in Canada so that we saw each other once a year. Despite the ocean separating us, she's had a big influence on me (not with cooking, though; she barely cooks). She doesn't speak English and my German was poor until a couple of years ago, but she tells me now that I would ask for two things, on repeat, whenever we were together. One, "Play Barbies"—which she hated—and two, "Muesli, please." My muesli is a slight spin on the simple everyday classic. It's in the spring chapter because strawberries are my Omi's favourite, but you can find seasonal variations below.

Omi's Muesli

Serves two | 5 minutes prep time | 2 hours chilling time

1¾ cups (400 ml) Coconut Yogurt (page 228)

1 teaspoon honey or maple syrup (optional)

1 cup (110 grams) rolled oats

½ cup (70 grams) seeds, (75 grams) chopped nuts, or (50 grams) shredded coconut

1 ripe banana, sliced

1 cup (200 grams) strawberries, hulled, with more for serving

1 teaspoon finely grated fresh ginger

Your favourite nut butter, for serving (optional)

Add all of the ingredients to a large bowl and mix with a wooden spoon. Cover and refrigerate for a minimum of 2 hours before serving with more fruit and a drizzle of nut butter (if using). This will keep well, refrigerated in a sealed container, for up to 3 days.

Seasonal Options:

Summer: stone fruits, berries, fresh ginger, edible flowers

Autumn: apples, pears, pomegranate, figs, cinnamon, nutmeg, dates

Winter: oranges, persimmons, bananas, pears, apples, frozen fruits, warm spices

GF | NF | SF | CE

A simple frittata or omelette is one of the easiest and healthiest vegetarian meals out there. I make a variation of this dish throughout the year, often when I need something speedy for dinner, but I like it as a weekend breakfast, too. Hearty and filling, it's just what you need to start off a busy day. This version is filled with spring vegetables and plenty of greens.

Leek Asparagus Frittata

Serves four | 10 minutes prep time | 25 minutes cooking time

6 large eggs

¼ cup (60 ml) non-dairy milk

1 teaspoon salt

1 teaspoon freshly ground pepper

2 teaspoons olive oil

1 leek, thinly sliced, dark greens discarded

1 bunch asparagus, ends trimmed and cut into 2-inch (5 cm) pieces

2 cloves garlic, minced

2 teaspoons thyme leaves

Preheat the oven to 400°F (200°C). Whisk together the eggs, milk, salt, and pepper. Set aside.

Heat a medium cast-iron pan or oven-safe skillet (about 8 inches / 20 cm; see note) over medium heat.

Add the oil to the frying pan, followed by the leek. Cook, stirring frequently, for 3 to 4 minutes. Add the asparagus, garlic, and thyme, and cook for another minute.

Pour the egg mixture into the pan. Place in the oven and bake for 15 to 20 minutes, or until the centre of the frittata is set. The cooking time may differ slightly depending on the size of your pan. This will keep well, refrigerated in a sealed container, for a couple of days, and reheats well.

NOTE

If you don't have an oven-safe skillet, cook the vegetables and then place them in a casserole dish before topping with the egg mixture and baking.

GF | NF | SF | YR

Lemon Coconut Bites

Makes about two dozen bites | 10 minutes prep time

The texture of these bites is phenomenal—like oatmeal cookie dough, chewy but not too soft—and they pack a little better than a standard date-based protein ball thanks to those rolled oats. Subtle lemon and coconut are reminiscent of cake, yet these are very lunchbox- and allergy-friendly, for school treats.

1 cup (100 grams) unsweetened shredded coconut (see note), plus more for coating (optional)

½ cup (55 grams) rolled oats

½ cup (70 grams) sunflower seeds

½ cup (120 grams) packed soft pitted dates

Zest of 1 lemon

Juice of 1 lemon

½ teaspoon vanilla extract

1 tablespoon non-dairy milk

In a food processor, pulse the coconut, oats, and sunflower seeds on high speed until a coarse meal forms. Add the dates, lemon zest, lemon juice, vanilla, and milk and blend until the mixture holds together when pressed.

Form the mixture into small balls, about 1 tablespoon each. After forming, the bites can be coated in the extra coconut, if you'd like. This helps to prevent them from sticking together but is optional. Refrigerate in a sealed container for up to 1 week, or freeze indefinitely.

NOTE

Flaked coconut can be used instead of shredded if you're out. Blend a little longer to get small enough pieces before adding the dates. However, it's best to use shredded coconut for coating the bites.

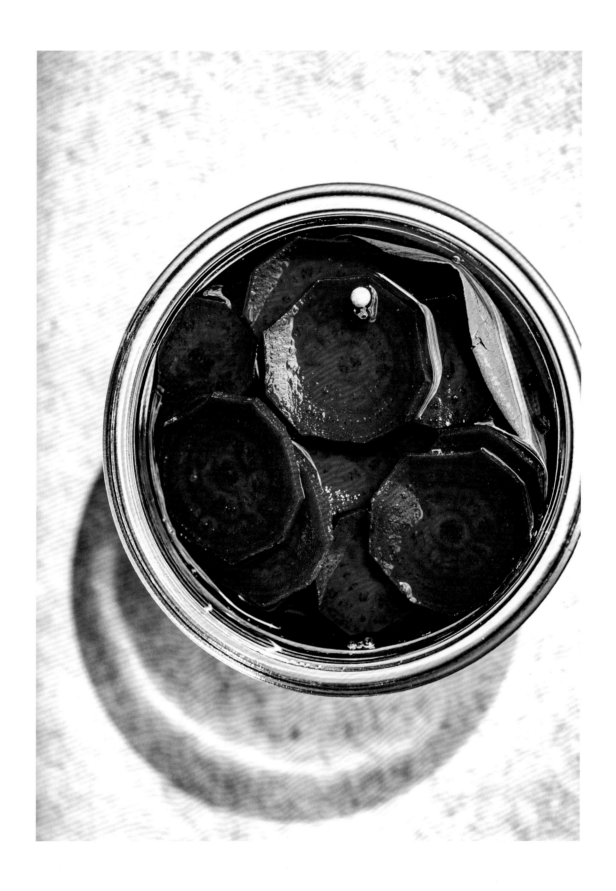

GF | NF

Quick Pickled Beets

Makes one or two jars, about 17 ounces (500 ml) total |
5 minutes prep time | 40 minutes cooking time | 2 hours resting time

I never liked pickled beets as a kid, but they've grown on me. On a burger, with crackers and dip—anywhere you need an extra bit of acidity and colour. I tried this recipe first with apple cider vinegar, which works well if you're using dark red beets. If you want to use yellow or Chioggia, though, apple cider vinegar will alter the colour and you'll lose their vibrancy. If you can get other varieties of beets, this recipe is particularly pretty with striped types, though the dark red is just as nice.

1 pound (500 grams) medium beets

½ cup (125 ml) white wine vinegar

3 tablespoons honey

6 peppercorns

¼ teaspoon salt

2 bay leaves

Preheat the oven to 375°F (190°C). Sterilize one or two lidded jars, totalling about 17 ounces (500 ml), with boiling water and set aside to dry.

Wash and trim the beets (don't peel them), then place them in a heavy-lidded dish. Roast for about 40 minutes, lid on, or until they can be easily pierced with a fork. Once the beets are cool enough to handle, slip the skins off with your fingers, and slice the beets as thinly as possible.

Whisk together the vinegar, honey, peppercorns, and salt. Place the bay leaves in the prepared jars. Layer the beets in the jars, then top with the vinegar mixture, making sure the beets are fully immersed.

Seal the jars and let them rest at room temperature for at least 2 hours before eating. They can be kept in the refrigerator for up to 2 weeks.

Vegetarian Charcuterie

Serves six | 20 minutes prep time | 10 minutes cooking time

Charcuterie is synonymous with meat, but it's much more interesting with vegetables. This is not a recipe so much as a concept for a party dish, but it also makes a really fun dinner— sort of a build-it-yourself meal. Several recipes from other chapters in the book are featured, and you can easily alter things to your preference. It's spring on a platter, and a slightly less intense version is a nice lunch. To make this fully vegan, just ditch the eggs.

7 ounces (200 grams) asparagus, ends trimmed

1 teaspoons olive oil

¼ teaspoon salt

4 large eggs

1 batch Coconut Labneh (page 231)

⅓ cup (20 grams) finely chopped mixed herbs (like mint, oregano, parsley, basil, chives)

1 teaspoon freshly ground pepper

1 batch Seed Crackers (page 177)

Quick Pickled Beets (page 31)

Strawberries

Radishes, halved

Handful snap peas

Preheat the oven to 400°F (200°C). Place the asparagus on a baking sheet, add the olive oil and the salt, and stir to coat. Roast for 8 to 10 minutes, or until the ends are crisp and golden.

While the asparagus is roasting, boil the eggs. For soft-boiled eggs, place the eggs in a pot and cover with cold water. Bring to a rolling boil over high heat, then reduce to low and simmer, covered, for 6 minutes. Drain and cover with cold water, then peel and halve to serve.

Roll the labneh into one or two balls, then coat in the herbs. Alternatively, roll into several small balls and serve in bowls.

Start to assemble the platter. On a large board or plate, arrange the roasted asparagus, boiled eggs, labneh balls, crackers, pickled beets, strawberries, radishes, and snap peas, keeping like colours separate for a more dramatic presentation. Sprinkle the eggs with pepper. Use small bowls when needed and incorporate them into the arrangement if you can.

Serve immediately. Most of the elements can be prepared ahead of time with the exception of the asparagus, so this dish can be put together quickly to serve to guests.

NF | YR

Spring Onion Biscuits

Makes eight biscuits | 10 minutes prep time | 20 minutes cooking time

While biscuits made with coconut oil are never going to be as fluffy as those made with butter or a good margarine, these are about as good as it gets. The dough, made with spelt flour, can quickly toughen when folded and rolled to form extra layers, so I've skipped that step here. As they're so quick to make, I can easily throw a batch together with soup or stew year-round (simply drop the spring onions when they're not in season). Absolutely best eaten fresh.

1 teaspoon apple cider vinegar

½ cup (125 ml) non-dairy milk

1½ cups (225 grams) light spelt flour

1 tablespoon coconut sugar

2 teaspoons baking powder

¼ teaspoon baking soda

1 teaspoon salt

¼ cup (60 grams) solid coconut oil

2 green or spring onions, chopped (see note)

Preheat the oven to 375°F (190°C) and line a baking sheet with parchment paper.

Whisk the vinegar into the milk and set aside.

Sift the flour, sugar, baking powder, baking soda, and salt into a large bowl. Use your hands or a pastry cutter to rub or cut in the coconut oil to form pea-sized crumbs. Stir in the spring onions, then use a wooden spoon to stir the milk mixture into the dry ingredients until just combined.

Form the dough into two equal discs, about 1½ inches (4 cm) thick. Cut each into four wedges. Place on the prepared baking sheet and bake for 18 to 20 minutes, or until golden. Serve warm, if you can. As with any biscuit, these are best eaten fresh, but will keep in a sealed container at room temperature for a couple of days.

NOTE

Spring onions and green onions are often used interchangeably, so feel free to use what you prefer or have on hand for this recipe.

GF | NF | YR

Spiced Strawberry Jam

Makes about 1½ cups (375 ml) | 5 minutes prep time |
10 minutes cooking time

*A touch of pink pepper and
ground coriander lift this jam out
of the ordinary and add a hint of
spice. Fresh or frozen strawberries
can be used in this recipe, so it
can easily be made year-round if
you're looking out of season. This
recipe is not suitable for canning,
as it's so lightly sweetened, but is
rather a nice low-effort jam that
can be prepared in a few minutes.*

2 cups (400 grams) strawberries

1 tablespoon water

1 tablespoon maple syrup

½ teaspoon vanilla extract

¼ teaspoon freshly ground pink pepper

¼ teaspoon coriander seeds, ground

Add all of the ingredients to a small saucepan and heat over medium-low heat. Bring to a simmer and cook for 8 to 10 minutes, stirring occasionally, until reduced and with a jam-like consistency. Store in the refrigerator for up to 1 week.

NF | CE

Bean and Herb Dumpling Soup

Serves four to six | 15 minutes prep time | 30 minutes cooking time

*Pesto, dumplings, and soup—
spring comfort food to the max.
The cooking time is surprisingly
short here and is more for the
dumplings than the soup itself.
Mixing both pesto and fresh basil
in the dumplings means they're
light and vibrant, and green peas
keep the simple soup fresh. I tried
baking the soup at the end to
finish the dumplings, but it didn't
make a difference. This recipe
was inspired by Heidi Swanson,
the queen of whole food cooking.*

Dumplings

1 large egg

½ cup (125 ml) non-dairy milk

4 tablespoons pesto, plus more
for serving (see note)

½ cup (30 grams) finely
chopped basil

1¼ cups (190 grams) spelt
flour

1 teaspoon coconut sugar

1 teaspoon baking powder

¼ teaspoon salt

Soup

1 teaspoon olive oil

1 small onion

2 medium carrots, halved
lengthwise and sliced into
½-inch (1 cm) pieces

2 cloves garlic, minced

2 tablespoons spelt flour

4 cups (1 litre) Vegetable Stock
(page 243)

1 teaspoon herbes de Provence

1 teaspoon salt

1 teaspoon freshly ground
pepper

2 cups (300 grams) cooked or
canned little white beans,
drained and rinsed

1 cup (150 grams) fresh or
frozen peas

To make the dumplings, beat the egg in a medium bowl. Whisk in the
milk, pesto, and basil. Add the flour, coconut sugar, baking powder,
and salt and stir to make a thick dough. Set aside.

For the soup, heat the oil in a large pot over medium heat. Once hot,
add the onions and sauté for 2 minutes, followed by the carrots for
another 5 minutes. Stir in the garlic and flour.

Pour in the stock and add the herbes de Provence, salt, and pepper.
Bring to a boil, then add the beans and reduce the heat to medium-
low. Simmer for 5 minutes, then stir in the peas.

Drop tablespoons of the dumpling mixture gently into the soup and
cook for 6 minutes. Gently flip the dumplings with a spoon and cook
for another 6 minutes, keeping the soup on a low simmer and covered.
Serve hot with extra pesto for each bowl.

NOTE
Either use prepared pesto or the recipe on page 97.

GF | NF | SF

Spring to a tee. All the green vegetables at their best in spring, lemon, and plenty of fresh herbs make this a light and refreshing soup. It's just right for those spring days that are chilly enough to warrant soup but you want something that's reflective of the season—that is, vibrantly green.

Spring Green Soup

Serves four to six | 10 minutes prep time | 40 minutes cooking time

1 teaspoon olive oil

1 small white onion, diced

3 cloves garlic, minced

1 teaspoon salt

1 teaspoon freshly ground pepper

½ teaspoon cayenne pepper

6 cups (1.5 litres) Vegetable Stock (page 243)

¾ cup (150 grams) dried Puy lentils (see note)

1 bay leaf

14 ounces (400 grams) asparagus, woody ends removed (see note)

1 cup (150 grams) fresh or frozen peas

3 cups (70 grams) spinach

Zest of 1 lemon

Juice of 1 lemon

1 cup (60 grams) finely chopped fresh basil, for serving

Heat the oil in a large pot over medium heat. Add the onions and sauté for 2 to 3 minutes, until softened and slightly browned. Stir in the garlic and cook another minute, then stir in the salt, pepper, and cayenne.

Pour in the vegetable stock, cover, and bring the soup to a rolling boil. Add the lentils and bay leaf. Reduce the heat and simmer for 20 to 25 minutes, or until the lentils are tender.

Add the asparagus and peas. Simmer, uncovered, for another 5 minutes. The asparagus should be bright green and still snappy. Remove from the heat and stir in the spinach, lemon zest, and lemon juice. Serve hot, topped with the herbs.

NOTES

If you want to, cut the asparagus into smaller pieces before cooking. It won't make a difference to the cooking time.

I have made this with pre-cooked lentils to reduce the cooking time to about 10 minutes total, but the flavour suffers and I recommend using dried lentils as written.

GF | NF

Potatoes are the best food, and new potatoes are even better. Potato salad should be one of the first things coming out of the kitchen as soon as new potatoes are ready in spring. Mustard and dill are a classic pairing, and lentils take the place of eggs here for a lighter, toothsome meal. Roasting the potatoes and tossing them in the vinaigrette while still warm are what make this dish. Don't let them cool first!

New Potato Salad

Serves four to six | 10 minutes prep time | 30 minutes cooking time

Salad

2½ pounds (1 kilogram) new potatoes

2 teaspoons olive oil

1 teaspoon salt

½ teaspoon freshly ground pepper

3 cups (70 grams) baby greens

2 cups (300 grams) cooked Puy lentils (see page 11)

Vinaigrette

¼ cup (60 ml) olive oil

3 tablespoons white wine vinegar

1 teaspoon Dijon mustard

½ teaspoon honey

½ teaspoon salt

½ teaspoon freshly ground pepper

¼ cup (15 grams) finely chopped dill

1 green onion, finely chopped

Preheat the oven to 400°F (200°C).

For the salad, cut the potatoes into roughly equal size if needed, and place on a large baking sheet. Add the oil, salt, and pepper, and toss to coat. Roast for 30 minutes, or until golden and crispy.

While the potatoes are roasting, make the vinaigrette. Add the oil, vinegar, mustard, honey, salt, and pepper to a jar or bowl and mix until fully combined. Stir in the dill and green onions, and set aside.

Place the roasted potatoes in a large heatproof bowl and add the greens and lentils. Stir in the vinaigrette and serve warm. This is best fresh, but can be refrigerated in a sealed container for up to 3 days.

GF | NF | SF

Persian Herb Salad

Serves two to four | 10 minutes prep time

For this salad, use a mix of herbs you enjoy. If you can find Persian basil, use it, but otherwise common Genovese basil is fine. I go light on cilantro and heavy on everything else—and other herbs, like parsley or oregano, are also nice here. If you have the time, let this salad sit for about half an hour before serving. It's not necessary, but mellows the onions and softens the overall flavour of the dish.

2 cups (300 grams) cooked or canned little white beans or chickpeas, drained and rinsed

1½ cups (90 grams) chopped mixed herbs, like cilantro, mint, chives, and basil

1 small red onion, very finely sliced

2 tablespoons sesame seeds

2 tablespoons olive oil

Zest of 1 lemon

Juice of 1 lemon

½ teaspoon salt

½ teaspoon freshly ground pepper

Add everything to a large bowl and mix well. Serve immediately at room temperature, or let it rest for 30 minutes to a couple of hours before serving. This keeps well, refrigerated, for up to 3 days.

NF | SF

Sautéed apricots are much easier than grilled, and adding a bit of colour concentrates their inherent sweetness. Mixing the sweet fruit with nutty freekeh, rich chickpeas, and a simple vinaigrette makes a truly perfect warm salad. Any leaf lettuce will work here, with escarole and arugula being particularly nice substitutions for Little Gem.

NOTES
If you, or your propensity to heartburn, have an aversion to raw onions, use some Pickled Red Onions (page 254) instead.

To make this gluten-free, use a grain like quinoa instead of freekeh.

Chickpea Apricot Grain Salad

Serves two | 10 minutes prep time | 40 minutes cooking time

Salad

⅓ cup (110 grams) freekeh

1 teaspoon olive oil

1 cup (150 grams) cooked or canned chickpeas, drained and rinsed

1 teaspoon sumac

¼ teaspoon salt

¼ teaspoon freshly ground pepper

8 apricots, halved and pitted

1 head Little Gem lettuce leaves

1 small red onion, very thinly sliced

Vinaigrette

2 tablespoons olive oil

1 tablespoon white wine vinegar

¼ teaspoon salt

¼ teaspoon freshly ground pepper

Add the freekeh to a lidded pot and cover with 1 cup (250 ml) well salted water. Bring to a boil, then reduce the heat and simmer, covered, for about 35 minutes, until tender, or about 20 minutes for white freekeh.

While the freekeh cooks, prepare the salad. Heat the oil in a large frying pan over medium heat. Add the chickpeas, sumac, salt, and pepper, and fry for 5 minutes, or until lightly golden and coated in the spices. Remove the chickpeas and set them aside, then put the pan back on the heat, keeping any residual oils and spices in the pan.

Place the apricots cut side down in the hot pan and cook for 2 minutes, or until lightly browned and softened, adding extra oil if needed.

For the vinaigrette, mix the oil, vinegar, salt, and pepper in a small jar or bowl until well combined.

To plate, arrange the lettuce on a large plate or platter, followed by the freekeh, chickpeas, apricots, and onions. Top with the vinaigrette and serve warm.

GF | NF | SF

Roasted Carrots with Black Lentils and Chermoula

Serves two to four | 10 minutes prep time | 30 minutes cooking time

This is based on a popular blog recipe I make a handful of times every month—with Chermoula (page 244) when there are enough herbs in the garden and my Basic Tahini Dressing (page 247) when there aren't. It started as a bare pantry meal, with basic ingredients like carrots and lentils making up the bulk of it, but it turned into a great weeknight dinner. The giant carrots often found in North American supermarkets should more likely be quartered instead of halved to keep to the suggested cooking time.

7 or 8 medium carrots, halved lengthwise

1 teaspoon olive oil

½ teaspoon salt, plus pinch for lentils

1 teaspoon Moroccan Spice Blend (page 248)

1 cup (150 grams) dried black (beluga) lentils, rinsed

2 cups (50 grams) arugula

¼ cup (60 ml) Chermoula (page 244)

Preheat the oven to 375°F (190°C).

Place the carrots on a large baking sheet and mix with the oil, salt, and spice blend. Keep them cut side up, as they tend to burn otherwise. Roast for 25 to 30 minutes, or until softened and golden.

While the carrots are cooking, prepare the lentils. Add the lentils to a medium pot, cover generously with water, add a pinch of salt, and bring to a boil. Reduce the heat and simmer, covered, for 20 to 25 minutes, or until tender. Strain any remaining water and set aside.

To assemble, arrange the arugula on a large plate or platter. Top with the lentils, then carrots, and finally chermoula. Serve warm. This can be refrigerated in a sealed container for a couple of days.

NF | SF

Nordic Burgers

Makes six burgers | 15 minutes prep time | 15 minutes cooking time |
30 minutes chilling time

*Traditional, old-school northern/
eastern European flavours—rye,
dill, beet, and sauerkraut—take
the forefront with these burgers.
Their texture is ultra-satisfying,
meaty, and solid, and they fry
well, but only if you use stale
bread. Although I avoid it for the
most part, avocado is consumed at
a shocking rate in Scandinavia—
especially Sweden—so I've
included it here despite it being
about as far from a classic Nordic
ingredient as you can get.*

NOTES

*Crusts or stale bread is an ideal
choice for this recipe. The
Scandinavian Dark Rye
(page 227) is just right after a
day or two on the counter.*

*To bake these, skip refrigerating
the burger mixture and bake the
patties at 350°F (180°C) for 25 to
30 minutes.*

Burgers

3 teaspoons olive oil, divided,
  plus more for frying

2 cups (200 grams) diced
  button mushrooms

1 medium onion, diced

1 medium leek, thinly sliced,
  dark greens discarded

2 cloves garlic, minced

½ cup (70 grams) sunflower
  seeds

½ cup (50 grams) stale rye
  bread cubes

1½ cups (225 grams) cooked
  brown lentils

⅓ cup (20 grams) dill

2 tablespoons apple cider
  vinegar

1 tablespoon Dijon mustard

1 teaspoon salt

½ teaspoon freshly ground
  pepper

½ teaspoon cayenne pepper

To Assemble

6 buns (rye is a nice choice)

Dill Pickle Sauerkraut
  (page 232)

Pickled Red Onions (page 254)

Avocado, sliced

Fresh dill

Heat 1 teaspoon olive oil in a large pan over medium heat. Sear the
mushrooms in the hot pan, avoiding stirring if possible, for 5 minutes.
Add the onions, leeks, and garlic and sauté for another 5 minutes, or
until softened and fragrant.

In the meantime, use a food processor to blend the sunflower seeds
and bread into a coarse meal. Add the cooked mushroom mixture, the
remaining 2 teaspoons olive oil, lentils, dill, vinegar, mustard, salt,
pepper, and cayenne. Pulse until a rough, crumbly texture forms—it
should hold together when pressed. Refrigerate for 30 minutes.

Once chilled, divide the mixture into six equal patties. Heat a large
frying pan over medium heat with a drizzle of olive oil. Fry the burgers
3 to 4 minutes each side, or until golden brown. Serve on buns and
top with sauerkraut, pickled onions, avocado, and dill.

NF

I made this recipe well over a dozen times while working on this book because I hated every round of photos. It was well worth it, let me tell you, because I still got to eat the pizza every time. I guarantee that it'll knock your socks off. I mean, pizza is one thing and this isn't that, but it's a round dough with stuff on it, so it is what it is. Green pizza, coming up. Spinach is called for twice in this recipe, in both the pesto and the toppings. Any hardy green, like chard, arugula, or kale, can be used in its place— whatever you have on hand.

Spring Pesto Pizza

Serves four | 30 minutes prep time | 25 minutes cooking time | 1 hour rising time

Dough

¼ cup (60 ml) warm water

1 teaspoon honey

2¼ teaspoons dry yeast (½ cube fresh)

1 cup (250 ml) water, room temperature

2 tablespoons olive oil, plus more for coating the bowl

2 teaspoons salt

2½ to 3 cups (375 to 450 grams) spelt flour, divided

Pesto

2 cups (50 grams) basil

1 cup (40 grams) packed spinach

1 clove garlic

Juice of 1 lemon

½ teaspoon salt

½ teaspoon freshly ground pepper

2 tablespoons olive oil

Toppings

4 cups (80 grams) spinach

14 ounces (400 grams) asparagus, halved lengthwise, woody ends removed

1 medium leek, cut into ½-inch (1 cm) rounds, dark greens discarded

1 medium zucchini, cut into ½-inch (1 cm) rounds

2 cups (200 grams) button mushrooms, cut into ½-inch (1 cm) slices

Olive oil, to drizzle

Pinch salt

To make the dough, whisk together the warm water, honey, and yeast in a large bowl. Let this mixture rest for 15 minutes. The yeast should bloom and look like foam (see note).

Stir in the room-temperature water, oil, salt, and 1 cup (150 grams) flour with a wooden spoon. Add the remaining flour about ½ cup (75 grams) at a time, stirring between each addition, until it becomes too difficult to mix.

Turn the dough out onto a well-floured surface. Knead for 5 to 10 minutes, sprinkling additional flour as needed, until a soft, smooth dough forms. If you have a stand mixer, skip hand kneading and use the dough hook in your mixer instead.

recipe continues . . .

Clean your bowl, then add a drizzle of olive oil to it. Place the dough in the bowl, turning to coat with the oil. Cover with a plate or tea towel and set in a warm, draft-free spot. Let the dough rise for 50 to 60 minutes, or until doubled in size.

While the dough is rising, make the pesto. Add the basil, spinach, garlic, lemon juice, salt, and pepper to a small food processor, or use an immersion blender, and blend well. Add the olive oil in a slow stream while blending, until fully incorporated and very smooth.

Preheat the oven to 400°F (200°C).

Divide the dough into two equal pieces, roll out into rough circles about 1 inch (2.5 cm) thick, and place on parchment paper.

To make the pizzas, top each round with equal amounts of the pesto. Reserve a couple of tablespoons for serving. Divide the toppings among the two rounds of dough, starting with the spinach at the base, followed by the asparagus, leek, zucchini, and mushrooms. Top each pizza with a drizzle of oil and sprinkle of salt.

Bake each pizza for 20 to 25 minutes, baking both at the same time if your oven has a convection setting. The vegetables should be tender and the crust golden. Top each pizza with a drizzle of pesto and serve hot. This is best fresh, but keeps well at room temperature for a day and is pretty good cold.

NOTES

A mix of about half light and half whole grain spelt flour is generally my choice, but you can use your preferred mix. Using all light spelt will result in a very light base more reminiscent of standard pizza.

If you mix together the warm water, honey, and yeast (step 1) and nothing seems to be happening (there's no foam), your yeast is likely dead, either from being too old or because you used too-hot water. Start again.

GF | SF

Chocolate Strawberry Milkshake

Serves one or two | 5 minutes prep time

Frozen banana adds creaminess to this smoothie, along with the hemp and nut and seed butter, making it more like a milkshake than a protein smoothie. Frozen strawberries work well, but fresh are excellent—just use what you have. This one is very kid-friendly.

2 cups (400 grams) hulled strawberries

1 frozen ripe banana

1 soft date, pitted (optional)

3 tablespoons hemp hearts

2 tablespoons raw cacao or cocoa powder

2 tablespoons chia seeds

2 tablespoons nut or seed butter

1 cup (250 ml) non-dairy milk

Add all of the ingredients to a blender and mix until smooth. Serve immediately.

GF | NF

Strawberry Elderflower Ginger Beer Floats

Serves two | 5 minutes prep time

My paternal aunt, who lived just up the road from us when I was growing up, made my sister and me floats a lot when we were little, most often with orange pop, and this recipe makes me think of her. But I love the idea of an ice cream float with fermented ginger beer and fruit-based ice cream instead of pop and sugary ice cream. It's a float minus the sugar headache.

8 strawberries, hulled

2 teaspoons elderflower blossoms

2 large scoops Strawberry Soft Serve (page 60) or another strawberry ice cream

2 cups (500 ml) Ginger Beer (page 215)

Use a fork to mash the strawberries with the elderflower blossoms. Divide equally into two glasses, then add a scoop of ice cream to each. Top with the ginger beer and serve immediately.

NOTE

If elderflower is out of season or you can't pick blossoms locally, there are a couple of alternatives. One, use a teaspoon of elderflower cordial in place of the blossoms. Two, use lilac blossoms instead for a more citrus-like, but still lightly floral, flavour.

GF | NF | SF

Sunrise Smoothie

Serves two | 5 minutes prep time

*Like mango lassi, swirled with
raspberries. Sweet mango,
coconut, and cardamom play off
slightly tart raspberries in this
smoothie, and swirling the
colours together makes for a very
pretty drink. I really like this in
spring when the light starts to
return, and it's possible again to
have breakfast while the sun is
rising—so, sunrise smoothie.*

1 ripe mango, peeled and cut into chunks (see note)

1 frozen ripe banana

1 soft date, pitted (optional)

Seeds of 1 cardamom pod

½ cup (125 ml) Coconut Yogurt (page 228)

½ cup (125 ml) non-dairy milk

¼ cup (50 grams) frozen raspberries

Add the mango, banana, date (if using), cardamom seeds, yogurt,
and milk to a blender and mix until smooth. Pour a quarter of the
smoothie into one glass and a quarter into another glass.

Add the raspberries to the remaining smoothie mixture and blend
again. Divide the raspberry mixture between the two glasses, and use
a spoon to swirl the colours. Serve immediately.

NOTES

*Frozen mango can be used instead of fresh. If you want to go that route, use
a fresh banana, as the smoothie will be too thick if both the mango and
banana are frozen.*

*If you really must, you can use ground cardamom here in place of the seeds,
but in a very small quantity—⅛ teaspoon or so, no more.*

GF | NF

Strawberry Soft Serve

Serves two to four | 5 minutes prep time

Ice cream cravings solved. I can't have ice cream in the house (I eat the whole tub in one sitting, no self-control whatsoever), but often have frozen strawberries and bananas. There are a lot of banana-based "ice cream" recipes out there, but adding a whack of coconut cream makes this actually taste like a fancy-ish soft serve. And this is coming from a person who worked in an ice cream shop for years—just saying.

1 frozen ripe banana

1 cup (200 grams) frozen strawberries

½ teaspoon vanilla extract

¼ cup (60 ml) coconut cream

1 teaspoon honey (optional)

Add all of the ingredients to a food processor or high-powered blender and blend for 3 to 5 minutes, until smooth. Serve immediately. This is best fresh, but it can be frozen in a sealed container for a couple of weeks. If you'd like to freeze it for later, thaw for 5 to 10 minutes at room temperature before serving.

NOTE
Coconut cream can simply be taken from the creamy top layer of a can of full-fat coconut milk.

NF

Rhubarb Berry Galette

Makes one large galette | 15 minutes prep time | 55 minutes cooking time

Galettes are pies' low-maintenance cousin and way more fun to make. Filling leaking? Don't worry about it. A bit uneven with the pastry? No problem. And coconut oil pastry is even easier than butter pastry, although, as usual with spelt, you do need to be careful not to overmix. Frozen raspberries are even better in this recipe than fresh, as they're sturdier when mixed with harder fruits.

Pastry

2 cups (300 grams) light spelt flour

2 tablespoons coconut sugar

½ teaspoon salt

¼ cup (60 grams) solid coconut oil (see note)

2 teaspoons vanilla extract

4 to 6 tablespoons cold water

Non-dairy milk, for brushing

Filling

6 stalks rhubarb, sliced into 1-inch (2.5 cm) pieces (about 5 cups / 500 grams)

1 cup (200 grams) halved strawberries

1 cup (200 grams) raspberries, fresh or frozen

3 tablespoons honey or maple syrup

1 teaspoon grated fresh ginger

1 teaspoon vanilla extract

Plain yogurt, ice cream, or Whipped Coconut Cream (page 256), for serving

In a large bowl, whisk together the flour, sugar, and salt. Use your hands or a pastry cutter to rub or cut in the coconut oil to form pea-sized crumbs. Add the vanilla, then the water 1 tablespoon at a time, stirring with a wooden spoon briefly between each addition. The pastry should be very slightly crumbly, but once enough water is added, it will hold together.

Form the pastry into a disc, cover with a bowl, and set aside while you prepare the filling.

To make the filling, add the rhubarb, strawberries, raspberries, honey, ginger, and vanilla to a large bowl and gently mix until well combined. Set aside.

Preheat the oven to 350°F (180°C) and line a large baking sheet with parchment paper.

On a well-floured surface, roll the pastry into a circle roughly 14 inches (35 cm) in diameter. Place on the baking sheet. Place the fruit filling in the centre of the pastry, then fold the pastry edges over the fruit. Brush the outside of the pastry with milk.

Bake for 50 to 55 minutes, or until the pastry is very golden. Cool for 10 minutes before serving with plain yogurt, ice cream, or whipped coconut cream.

NOTE
If your coconut oil is on the softer side of solid, you'll end up using much less water and sacrifice pastry structure. Measure it out and then refrigerate until hard before adding to the pastry.

NF

Oil-based, eggless cakes are a dream to make—no creaming sugar and butter, or beating eggs, or electric mixing required (the whipped cream is exempt). This cake has a nice lemon flavour and is easy to put together, despite the glamour of the finished cake. The recipe was doubled to make the pictured cake, but I thought such a large cake might be a bit much for average needs. Double the recipe if you need a very large, statuesque cake. It makes a lovely small wedding cake—it was mine!

NOTE
This can be topped with edible flowers, such as lilac blossoms, elderflower blossoms, and pansies. The flowers pictured are not edible and were removed before serving.

Lemon Vanilla Layer Cake

Makes one 2-layer cake | 15 minutes prep time | 55 minutes cooking time

Cake

2½ cups (375 grams) light spelt flour

½ cup (80 grams) coconut sugar

2 teaspoons baking powder

½ teaspoon baking soda

½ teaspoon salt

1¼ cups (300 ml) non-dairy milk

½ cup (125 ml) olive oil

Zest of 2 lemons

Juice of 1 lemon

2 teaspoons vanilla extract

Topping

1 batch Whipped Coconut Cream (page 256)

2 tablespoons runny honey

Zest of 1 lemon

2 tablespoons lemon juice

2 cups (400 grams) strawberries

Preheat the oven to 350°F (180°C) and grease an 8-inch (20 cm) springform pan with coconut oil.

Whisk together the flour, sugar, baking powder, baking soda, and salt in a large bowl. In a smaller bowl, mix the milk, oil, lemon zest, lemon juice, and vanilla. Add the wet ingredients to the dry ingredients and stir until just combined.

Pour the batter into the prepared pan and bake for 50 to 55 minutes, or until golden and a toothpick inserted into the middle of the cake comes out clean. Remove from the oven and cool on a rack before removing from the pan and cooling fully before assembling.

To assemble the cake, cut it into two equal layers. Spread half of the whipped coconut cream between the layers, and the remaining cream over the outside of the cake. To make the layers as pictured, use an offset spatula to gently scrape the sides of the cake to remove any excess cream.

Mix the honey, lemon zest, and lemon juice in a small bowl. Top the cake with the strawberries, then drizzle with the lemon honey mixture. Serve immediately. Leftovers can be refrigerated and will keep well, covered, for up to 3 days, but the cream will harden and soak into the cake slightly.

Summer

Food in summer is marked by a bounty of tomatoes, stone fruits, and salads. I understand that no one really likes to cook in the summer and it can become more of a chore than anything. I wrote the vast majority of this book over the hottest summer on record in the Netherlands, and let me tell you, it was a grouchy season. With temperatures soaring past 40°C (105°F) and the oven on, I quickly learned that Dutch houses are not built for heat.

A handful of recipes in this chapter need an oven, but most were made with the hot weather in mind, with a shortened cooking or baking time. There will always be cool and rainy days, even in summer (hopefully, at least, as climate change wreaks havoc on previous norms), so a couple of recipes reflect that—the summer minestrone and pesto vegetable tart are both ideal for cooler summer weather. Mostly, the time needed in the kitchen is brief, because we have better things to do than cook when it's warm outside. Even the cooked recipes can be eaten at room temperature to avoid reheating, and they are all very good cold, with perhaps the exception of the minestrone.

This is a picnic- and outdoor-eating-friendly chapter, partly because there's little I hate more than being stuck indoors in summer, and partly because that's what people are doing at this time of year. So cook some pakoras in the cool evening, then pack them to bring to a lake the next day with some raita and a fun salad.

I always get the feeling that I've missed the best of summer food, because I'd much rather go to the beach than be in the kitchen, but the goal of this chapter is to help you achieve both. Enjoy the seasonal abundance—but don't take too much time cooking it.

NF | SF | CE

Harissa French Toast

Serves two or three | 5 minutes prep time | 10 minutes cooking time

French toast is nothing new, but the spice of harissa paired with the richness of the eggs makes this savoury version feel like a revelation. If you want to use a bread recipe from this book here, the spelt sourdough is good for French toast, while the dark rye is not. A brioche or plain challah— something that will absorb more of the egg mix (but is definitely a bit more on the decadent side)—is ideal. I always think of hot weather as the right time to embrace spicier food, and this does the trick.

Olive oil

3 large eggs

1 cup (250 ml) non-dairy milk

2 teaspoons Harissa (page 244)

½ teaspoon salt

Six 1-inch (2.5 cm) slices soft bread

Toppings

2 or 3 eggs (1 egg per person), fried or poached

1 cup (150 grams) halved cherry tomatoes

¼ cup (60 ml) Chermoula (page 244)

Heat a large skillet over medium heat with a drizzle of olive oil.

In a shallow bowl, whisk the eggs well. Stir in the milk, harissa, and salt. Dip the bread into the egg mixture, leaving each side to sit in the bowl for at least 30 seconds.

Fry the soaked bread slices for 2 to 3 minutes each side, until golden. While the toasts are cooking, prepare the poached or fried eggs.

Make stacks of two to three pieces of toast for each person. Top each stack with an egg, a handful of tomatoes, and a drizzle of chermoula. Serve immediately.

GF | YR

Even though this is, in essence, a chia pudding, it really is deluxe, thanks to the coconut milk. And does it ever make a difference. A little fresh ginger and vanilla boost this breakfast even more, along with all the fresh fruits you can get your hands on. Although I provide the toppings in the recipe as pictured, the base for these bowls can be topped with anything you like: cinnamon apples in autumn, oranges and persimmons in winter, elderflower or lilacs and early berries in spring.

Deluxe Breakfast Bowls

Serves two | 5 minutes prep time | 2 hours chilling time

1 cup (250 ml) light coconut milk

3 tablespoons chia seeds

1 teaspoon maple syrup

½ teaspoon grated fresh ginger

½ teaspoon vanilla extract

Toppings

1 nectarine, pitted and sliced

1 plum, pitted and sliced

4 cherries, pitted

5 to 6 strawberries, hulled if desired

2 tablespoons pumpkin seeds

Almond butter, to drizzle

In a medium bowl or container, whisk together the coconut milk, chia, maple syrup, ginger, and vanilla. Cover and refrigerate for at least 2 hours, or overnight.

To serve, stir the chia pudding to loosen. Split it between two bowls and top with the nectarines, plums, cherries, strawberries, pumpkin seeds, and almond butter. Serve immediately or refrigerate for up to 3 days in a sealed container.

GF

Sweet Hummus with Summer Fruits

Serves four to six | 20 minutes prep time

A loose definition of hummus, although this sweet version isn't that far off, apart from a bit of honey and different spices. While I like this best with piles of fruit, as pictured, I also use it as a bread spread, a topping for breakfast bowls, and sometimes even a dip for cookies. Serving this at a summer get-together or picnic with all the fruit is a gorgeous option. A generous prep time is given here, despite the dip itself needing only about 2 minutes. Prepping all that fruit takes time!

Hummus

¾ cup (110 grams) cooked or canned chickpeas, drained and rinsed

½ cup (125 ml) Coconut Yogurt (page 228)

2 tablespoons honey

1 tablespoon tahini or nut butter

½ teaspoon vanilla extract

¼ teaspoon freshly ground pink pepper

¼ teaspoon rosewater

Zest of 1 lemon

Summer Fruits

2 cups (400 grams) strawberries, hulled

4 peaches, pitted and sliced

2 nectarines, pitted and sliced

4 plums, pitted and sliced

1 cup (200 grams) cherries

To make the hummus, place the chickpeas, yogurt, honey, tahini, vanilla, pepper, rosewater, and lemon zest in a food processor and blend until very smooth.

To serve, arrange the strawberries, peaches, nectarines, plums, and cherries on a large platter or board with a bowl of the hummus. Any leftovers will keep well in the refrigerator for up to 3 days.

NOTES

Tahini ties into the flavours of pink pepper and rosewater, but if you're making this for kids or someone with a real sweet tooth, choose a sweeter nut or seed butter instead of the tahini. Cashew and almond butter are great.

Rosewater can be found at any Indian or South Asian specialty store or purchased online. A small bottle will last a long time—just make sure it's labelled for cooking and not skincare.

If you prefer, the cherries can be pitted before plating.

GF

Blueberry Nut Butter Cookies

Makes ten cookies | 5 minutes prep time | 10 minutes cooking time

This is an extraordinarily simple recipe, exactly what I look for in the summertime. It makes the best chewy cookie, without any leavening agent needed, or wheat, or eggs. Blueberries are lovely in these, both delicious and attractive—but if they're out of season for you, just use chocolate!

¾ cup (150 grams) Nut and Seed Butter (page 240)

¼ cup (60 ml) maple syrup

¼ cup (40 grams) coconut flour

1 tablespoon olive oil

1 teaspoon vanilla extract

1 teaspoon cinnamon

½ teaspoon salt

½ cup (100 grams) fresh blueberries

Preheat the oven to 350°F (180°C) and line a baking sheet with parchment paper.

Mix the nut and seed butter, maple syrup, coconut flour, oil, vanilla, cinnamon, and salt in a large bowl. Stir with a wooden spoon until thickened, about 30 seconds. Gently fold in the blueberries. It will be a stiff dough.

Form the cookie dough into ten small balls and place on the baking sheet. Gently flatten into discs. Bake for 8 to 10 minutes, or until golden. Cool for 10 minutes before removing from the sheet and cooling fully on a rack. These are best kept in a sealed container in the refrigerator or another cool place, for up to 3 days, as the berries will spoil quickly at room temperature.

NOTES

Frozen blueberries equal very purple cookies. You can use them—the taste is the same—but they will colour the dough.

Peanut or almond butter are delicious in this recipe.

Occasionally Eggs

Sweet Corn and Zucchini Pakora

Serves two to four | 10 minutes prep time | 10 minutes cooking time

These may not be deep-fried like in a traditional recipe, but the flavour is excellent. They offer a true taste of summer and, with all that chickpea flour, are surprisingly filling. A little spicy, with some sweetness from the corn, they are excellent with raita and are just as good served cold at a picnic or made in advance when the days are too hot to cook.

1 medium zucchini, grated (about 1 cup / 100 grams)

1 cup (150 grams) sweet corn

1 cup (30 grams) finely chopped spinach

¼ cup (15 grams) finely chopped parsley

1 small yellow onion, grated (about ¼ cup / 30 grams)

1 clove garlic, minced

1 teaspoon grated fresh ginger

2 tablespoons olive oil, plus more for cooking

2 tablespoons water

¾ cup (90 grams) chickpea flour

1 teaspoon salt

1 teaspoon ground turmeric

½ teaspoon cumin seeds

½ teaspoon cayenne pepper

¼ teaspoon baking powder

Coconut Yogurt Raita (page 82), for serving

Add the zucchini, corn, spinach, parsley, onions, garlic, ginger, oil, water, chickpea flour, salt, turmeric, cumin, cayenne, and baking powder to a large bowl and use your hands to mix until fully combined. There shouldn't be any streaks of flour remaining.

Heat a large frying pan over medium heat. Add a tablespoon of olive oil to the pan and then place 2 tablespoons of batter in the pan for each pakora. Fry for 2 minutes each side, until golden. When flipping, use a spatula to flatten the patties to about ½ inch (1 cm) thick. Repeat until all of the batter has been used, adding more oil to the pan as needed.

Serve hot with raita, or at room temperature. They will keep well at room temperature for a day or two and can be refrigerated in a sealed container for up to 3 days.

NOTE
Alternatively, these can be baked at 425°F (220°C) for about 25 minutes, until golden. Fried is better, though.

NF

Honey Thyme Crostini

Serves two to four | 5 minutes prep time | 5 minutes cooking time

Simple but effective: a dressed-up toast for summer, which I imagine you'll eat while wandering through your formal garden in a large hat. Most of us will eat this in front of our computers, but it'll feel like we're doing something much fancier.

½ loaf Basic Spelt Sourdough (page 223) or 1 baguette

Zest of 1 lemon

2 tablespoons thyme leaves

1 batch Coconut Labneh (page 231)

4 peaches, pitted and thinly sliced

A couple of twists of freshly ground black pepper

Honey, to drizzle

Olive oil, to drizzle

Slice the bread into ¾-inch (2 cm) slices. Toast until golden, either in a toaster or in a lightly oiled frying pan over medium heat.

Mix the lemon zest and thyme into the labneh. Spread each slice of bread with a thick layer of the lemon thyme labneh, then top with several peach slices. Top each with a sprinkle of pepper and a drizzle of honey and olive oil. Serve warm if you can.

GF | NF | SF

Peach Guacamole

Serves four as a side | 5 minutes prep time

Stone fruits are delicious in savoury dishes, but this is often overlooked in favour of using them in pies and other sweets. Peaches add a sweet element to this guacamole, making it even better for topping a taco or serving with chips in the summer. The lime keeps the avocado fresh for a while, so you can make this a couple of hours ahead of time without worrying about ugly guacamole.

2 ripe peaches, pitted and diced

2 ripe avocados, peeled, pitted, and diced

½ small red onion, finely chopped (about 3 tablespoons)

1 small jalapeño pepper, minced

2 tablespoons finely chopped cilantro

Juice of 1 lime

½ teaspoon salt

Add all of the ingredients to a bowl and mix well. Add more lime juice or salt to taste and serve immediately. If you want to make this a couple of hours in advance, keep it in a sealed container at room temperature. Any longer than 2 to 3 hours and the peaches will start to break down.

GF | NF | SF

Coconut Yogurt Raita

Serves four as a side | 5 minutes prep time

Raita is one of the best foods ever invented, and I've been obsessed with it since I was a little kid. Naan and raita were easily within my top five right from when I was about six years old, up until yogurt became a no-go a few years ago. Since then, I've lived a desperate and miserable raita-free existence—until now. Coconut yogurt is an ideal choice, and if you've never tried this cooling yogurt dish, you've been missing out. To make this even thicker, use the labneh option. Serve alongside any spicy dish, like the Sweet Corn and Zucchini Pakora (page 77) or Yoga Bowl (page 93).

½ cup (60 grams) grated cucumber

1 cup (250 ml) Coconut Yogurt (page 228) or Coconut Labneh (page 231)

¼ cup (15 grams) finely chopped cilantro

¼ cup (15 grams) finely chopped mint

¼ teaspoon cumin seeds

¼ teaspoon salt

Place the grated cucumber in a fine-mesh sieve and squeeze to remove excess water. Set aside.

Stir together the yogurt, cilantro, mint, cumin, and salt in a bowl. Fold in the cucumber and serve. Raita will keep well, refrigerated, for up to 3 days.

NOTE
Generally, a dense, low-seed cucumber like a Suyo or Persian is preferable to English in raita, but specifying that feels snobbish—especially since I can't get them where I live unless I grow them myself. If you can get or grow them, try them, and if not, use whichever variety you have on hand.

NF | SF

To someone from a cold climate, anything Italian feels like it belongs only in summer, and this soup fits the bill. It isn't that far off from what's often associated with minestrone. A northern Italian friend once told me that it's not minestrone unless you can stand your spoon up in it, but we're not adhering to that rule. This soup takes advantage of the best of high summer, with zucchini, eggplant, green beans, and corn.

NOTES
Feel free to sub diced fresh tomatoes for canned here.

As in any noodle soup, the pasta tends to soak up all available broth and turn into a carb-laden mess if left to its own devices. If you know you'll have leftovers, cook the pasta separately and add it to the soup when serving instead. To do this, reduce the vegetable stock by 1 cup (250 ml), and simply simmer for an additional 5 minutes with the beans and corn instead of returning to a boil (in step 4).

Summer Minestrone

Serves four to six | 10 minutes prep time | 30 minutes cooking time

1 teaspoon olive oil

1 medium red onion, diced

1 medium zucchini, cut into ¾-inch (2 cm) pieces

1 medium eggplant, cut into ¾-inch (2 cm) pieces

3 cloves garlic, minced

1 teaspoon salt

½ teaspoon cayenne pepper

½ teaspoon freshly ground pepper

1 teaspoon balsamic vinegar

1 can (13½ ounces / 400 grams) diced or whole tomatoes

6 cups (1.5 litres) Vegetable Stock (page 243)

1 bay leaf

1½ cups (225 grams) cooked or canned kidney beans, drained and rinsed

1½ cups (100 grams) short pasta (like fusilli or macaroni)

1 cup (150 grams) halved green beans

1 cup (150 grams) sweet corn

¼ cup (15 grams) chopped oregano

¼ cup (15 grams) chopped basil

Heat the olive oil in a large pot over medium heat.

Sauté the onions for 2 minutes, until slightly softened. Add the zucchini and eggplant and cook for another 3 to 4 minutes, stirring regularly, until lightly browned. Add the garlic, cook for another minute, then stir in the salt, cayenne, and pepper.

Add the vinegar, followed by the tomatoes, vegetable stock, and bay leaf. Bring to a boil, then reduce the heat and simmer for 10 minutes, covered.

Increase the heat to high and bring back to a rolling boil, then add the kidney beans and pasta. Cook the pasta according to package instructions, about 10 minutes, adding the green beans and corn halfway through.

Remove the pot from the heat and stir in the oregano and basil. Taste and season as necessary, and serve hot. Leftovers, without the pasta (see note), keep well in a sealed container in the refrigerator for up to 3 days, or can be frozen for up to a month.

NF | SF | YR

Lentil Harira

Serves four to six | 10 minutes prep time | 30 minutes cooking time

Harira is a traditional Moroccan lentil soup, often served during Ramadan, with a plethora of variations. I know you might not think that a lentil soup is an appropriate summer soup, but this one has a short cooking time and is absolutely worthwhile, even when it's warm. I make this soup year-round with seasonal substitutions—often nothing more than changing out the eggplant for something like pumpkin—but I do like it very much during the cool, wet summer days that are so common in northern Europe. It is exceptionally simple to prepare but has a deeply complex flavour.

2 teaspoons olive oil

1 small yellow onion, diced

2 medium carrots, quartered lengthwise and cut into ½-inch (1 cm) pieces

1 medium eggplant, cut into 1-inch (2.5 cm) pieces

2 cloves garlic, minced

1 teaspoon ground turmeric

1 teaspoon cumin seeds

1 teaspoon cinnamon

1 teaspoon salt

½ teaspoon freshly ground pepper

½ teaspoon cayenne pepper

1 can (13½ ounces / 400 grams) diced tomatoes

1 litre (4 cups) Vegetable Stock (page 243)

¾ cup (150 grams) dried red lentils

Juice of 1 lemon

Chopped cilantro, for serving

Basic Spelt Sourdough (page 223), Garlic Spelt Naan (page 178), or brown rice, for serving

Heat the oil in a large pot over medium heat.

Add the onions and sauté for 2 minutes, until softened and fragrant. Add the carrots and eggplant and cook for another 4 to 5 minutes to lightly brown.

Stir in the garlic, turmeric, cumin, cinnamon, salt, pepper, and cayenne. Add the tomatoes and vegetable stock and bring to a rolling boil, then add the lentils and reduce to a simmer. Cover and cook for 15 to 20 minutes, or until the lentils are cooked and the carrots are tender.

Remove from the heat and stir in the lemon juice, then taste and season if needed. Serve hot with the cilantro and some sourdough, naan, or brown rice, if you're into that. Leftovers keep very well in sealed containers in the refrigerator for up to 3 to 4 days, or in the freezer for up to a couple of months, with minimal change in taste or texture.

GF | NF | SF

Cucumber Melon Salad with Herbs

Serves two to four as a side | 10 minutes prep time

Cucumbers and watermelon are the middle children of summer produce, overlooked and ignored in favour of stone fruits and tomatoes. They shouldn't be. Just as exciting as the more glamorous produce, with many varieties and an abundance of colours and textures, they're so much more than forgotten sides at a barbeque. This is a highly hydrating salad with a dazzling blend of herbs, something you'll want to make on every hot day that comes your way.

1 large English cucumber, cut into 1-inch (2.5 cm) pieces

½ medium watermelon, cut into 1-inch (2.5 cm) pieces

¼ cup (10 grams) thyme leaves

¼ cup (10 grams) dill

¼ cup (10 grams) oregano

3 tablespoons olive oil

1 tablespoon white balsamic or wine vinegar

¼ teaspoon salt

¼ teaspoon freshly ground pepper

Place all of the ingredients in a large bowl, mix well, and serve. This will keep well, refrigerated, for a day or two in a sealed container.

NF | SF

Yes, right after I've touted the brilliance of summer cucumbers and melon, here is a tomato salad. Delicious, simple, and a way to use some of the tomatoes that take over in late July and August. Bread in salad is always a good idea, and this is no exception. Slightly stale sourdough soaks up some of the tomato juice, turning both crispy and soft, and is all-around excellent.

Mediterranean Tomato Salad

Serves two to four | 10 minutes prep time

Tomato Salad

6 large tomatoes, sliced, or a mix of cherry tomatoes

1 small red onion, sliced very thinly

½ cup (30 grams) chopped basil

2 tablespoons oregano leaves

2 tablespoons thyme leaves

1 Basic Spelt Sourdough (page 223), sliced, toasted, and torn into pieces

Vinaigrette

3 tablespoons olive oil

1 tablespoon balsamic vinegar

1 teaspoon sumac

½ teaspoon freshly ground pepper

¼ teaspoon salt

Scatter the tomatoes, onions, basil, oregano, thyme, and bread pieces on a platter or mix in a large bowl.

To make the vinaigrette, whisk the oil, vinegar, sumac, pepper, and salt in a small bowl. Pour over the salad and serve immediately.

To make this ahead or to store, mix the salad without the bread and add bread just before serving. It will keep well for a day at room temperature, as fresh summer tomatoes really shouldn't be refrigerated.

NOTE

A mix of different colours and varieties of tomatoes is both tasty and pretty in this salad, but all tomatoes taste good in summertime.

NF | SF

This isn't a regular old green salad—it's more of a meal in a bowl, with both chickpeas and lentils adding oodles of protein. The mango keeps everything light in this otherwise very green and legume-heavy dish, naan gives heft, and raita levels it. Try this for a very nice work lunch or light dinner.

Yoga Bowl

Serves two | 10 minutes prep time | 10 minutes cooking time

Curry Roasted Chickpeas

1 cup (150 grams) cooked or canned chickpeas, drained and rinsed

1 teaspoon olive oil

½ teaspoon salt

1 teaspoon Curry Spice Blend (page 248) or garam masala

For Assembly

1 cup (150 grams) cooked black (beluga) lentils, drained and rinsed

Juice of 1 lemon

¼ cup (15 grams) chopped cilantro

¼ teaspoon salt

2 cups (50 grams) baby spinach

1 mango, peeled and cut into strips

1 English cucumber, cut into spears

¼ cup (60 grams) Coconut Yogurt Raita (page 82)

2 pieces Garlic Spelt Naan (page 178), toasted

To make the chickpeas, heat a large frying pan over medium heat. When the pan is hot, add the chickpeas, oil, salt, and spice blend. Stirring occasionally, cook until the chickpeas are browned and slightly crunchy, about 5 minutes. Set aside.

In a separate bowl, mix the black lentils, lemon juice, cilantro, and salt.

To assemble the bowls, divide the spinach between two bowls. Top with the lentils, chickpeas, mangoes, cucumbers, raita, and toasted naan. To pack for lunches or as leftovers, keep the bread separate from the rest of the salad until serving. Without the bread, the salad will keep well in the refrigerator for a couple of days in an airtight container.

NF | SF

This recipe was an absolute treasure while I was working on this book. With the hottest summer on record in the Netherlands, cooking was often a bit of a nightmare, and this simple pasta, with such a short prep and cooking time, kept me sane. Mixing the salad while the pasta is hot wilts the spinach and warms everything slightly. The end result is a dish that's room temperature, rather than hot—much better for summer days. I love packing this for lunch or trips—it holds up well, even if stuck in a warm backpack all day.

Lazy Tomato Peach Pasta

Serves four | 10 minutes prep time | 10 minutes cooking time

3½ cups (250 grams) short pasta (such as fusilli, farfalle, or cavatappi)

2 cups (300 grams) halved cherry tomatoes

1 cup (150 grams) cooked or canned large white beans, drained and rinsed

2 peaches, pitted and sliced

2 cups (50 grams) baby spinach

½ cup (20 grams) basil

3 tablespoons olive oil

Juice of 1 lemon

½ teaspoon salt

½ teaspoon freshly ground pepper

Cook the pasta in well-seasoned water according to package instructions.

Place the cooked pasta in a large bowl. Add the tomatoes, beans, peaches, and spinach. Tear the basil into the bowl. Top with the oil, lemon juice, salt, and pepper, and mix well. Serve warm or at room temperature. This will keep well, refrigerated, for up to 3 days in an airtight container.

Pesto Vegetable Tart

Makes one large tart | 30 minutes prep time | 55 minutes cooking time

Striking in appearance but with simple summer ingredients, this vegetable tart is a true centrepiece dish. An easy press-in pastry with buttery almond flour, almond butter pesto, and the best hot-weather veg make for a robustly flavoured meal. This makes a great picnic dish and tastes just as good at room temperature as it does fresh out of the oven.

Pastry

1¾ cups (260 grams) spelt flour

½ cup (50 grams) almond flour

¾ teaspoon salt

¼ cup (60 grams) solid coconut oil

4 to 6 tablespoons cold water

Almond Butter Pesto

2 cups (60 grams) basil

2 cloves garlic

Juice of 1 lemon

2 tablespoons almond butter

½ teaspoon salt

3 tablespoons olive oil

Vegetable Filling

1 green zucchini

1 yellow zucchini

1 medium eggplant

1 small red onion

2 medium potatoes

2 plum tomatoes

Grease a 10-inch (25 cm) tart tin with coconut oil.

To make the pastry, mix the spelt flour, almond flour, and salt in a large bowl. Use your hands or a pastry cutter to rub or cut in the coconut oil to form pea-sized crumbs. Stir in the water 1 tablespoon at a time, until the dough holds its form when pressed.

On a well-floured work surface, roll the pastry into a rough circle ⅕ inch (5 mm) thick. Carefully place in the tart tin and gently press into the form. Trim any overhanging pastry and set the tin to the side.

For the pesto, add the basil, garlic, lemon juice, almond butter, and salt to a tall container and blend with an immersion blender until finely chopped. Add the oil in a slow stream, blending, until fully combined and the mixture is a paler green. Alternatively, you can use a small blender or food processor. Spoon ½ cup (125 ml) of the pesto onto the base of the pastry and spread into an even layer.

To make the filling, very thinly slice all of the vegetables into rounds (see note). Use a mandoline if you have one. Place on the pastry in concentric circles, alternating vegetables for varied colour.

Bake for 50 to 55 minutes, or until golden brown and the vegetables are slightly crisped. Serve hot or at room temperature. Leftovers can be refrigerated in a sealed container for up to 3 days.

NOTE

Although this is photographed with the vegetables sliced and arranged in spiral form, which is admittedly beautiful, I often make this recipe by chopping the vegetables into haphazard chunks and tossing them into the pastry shell instead. If you're not looking to impress anyone, take this much simpler route—the taste is almost the same. The prep time reflects the extra time needed for the arrangement, so if you're not keen on doing the design, it won't take nearly as long.

GF | NF | SF

Roasted Ratatouille with Quinoa

Serves four | 10 minutes prep time | 50 minutes cooking time

I started making this when Graham and I first moved to Germany. We initially lived in an apartment just a couple of blocks away from the largest market in the city, and we did most of our grocery shopping there. It was late summer, so all of these ingredients were at their peak. Roasted and served over a bit of quinoa, it's a great simple meal, and how I most love to serve this riff on ratatouille, but you could use any grain, or pasta, or bread, or simply chickpeas.

2 small red onions, cut into wedges

5 cloves garlic, thinly sliced

2 small eggplants, halved lengthwise and cut into ¾-inch (2 cm) slices

2 small zucchinis, halved lengthwise and cut into ¾-inch (2 cm) slices

2 red peppers, cut into 1-inch (2.5 cm) pieces

2 cups (300 grams) cherry tomatoes

2 tablespoons olive oil

2 tablespoons balsamic vinegar

4 sprigs thyme, leaves only

2 tablespoons finely chopped oregano, plus more for serving

2 cups (200 grams) cooked quinoa (see page 11)

Preheat the oven to 375°F (190°C).

Place the red onions, garlic, eggplants, zucchinis, red peppers, tomatoes, oil, vinegar, thyme, and oregano in a large casserole dish or on a rimmed baking sheet. Stir well to mix.

Bake the vegetables for 40 to 50 minutes, or until softened and with darker edges. While the vegetables are roasting, cook the quinoa if it hasn't been cooked ahead of time.

Serve the vegetables hot over the prepared quinoa, topped with additional oregano. This keeps well in a sealed container, refrigerated, for up to 3 days and reheats well.

GF | NF

Rehydration Smoothie

Serves four | 5 minutes prep time

For this smoothie, it's important that at least one of your main ingredients is frozen before you start, or that you add ice when blending. If everything is fresh, the blender tends to warm it up a bit and no one wants that when heat is the enemy. Spinach is likely the easiest, since you probably already have it in your freezer, but I usually forget and pop in a bit of ice instead. It's a pleasantly mild green smoothie—a nice starter green smoothie—and a good way to get some fruit and veg in. Just lightly sweet, but very hydrating, it's great to have after a workout or on an especially hot day.

1 large English cucumber, chopped

½ honeydew melon, chopped and rind removed

1 cup (25 grams) baby spinach

4 to 5 mint leaves (see note)

1 cup (250 ml) coconut water

Juice of 1 lime

1 teaspoon honey (optional)

3 to 4 ice cubes (optional)

Add all of the ingredients to a blender or use an immersion blender to mix until smooth. Serve immediately.

NOTE
Spearmint is milder than peppermint and is ideal for this smoothie, but peppermint is good too, if a bit strong. Use what you have.

Occasionally Eggs

GF | NF

Watermelon Refresher

Serves four | 5 minutes prep time

This drink is a summer staple, and I don't think I've gone a season without it since learning how to use a blender. A bit like a lemonade, a bit like a fruit daiquiri minus the rum (although if you're going to add liquor, go with rum), a bit like the best thing you can make when the sun is out.

¼ large watermelon, chopped (about 5 pounds / 2 kilograms)

2 cups (400 grams) frozen raspberries

Juice of 1 lemon

1 tablespoon honey (optional)

Add all of the ingredients to a blender and mix on high speed until smooth. Serve immediately.

NOTE
Add two shots of light rum to the mix to make this into a blended cocktail.

Blackberry Kombucha Sparkler

Serves two | 5 minutes prep time

I live in a region where blackberries grow wild on the roadside, positively everywhere, and it's easily been one of the best things about moving to a different climate. Blackberries are tolerant of poor growing conditions and can be found wild almost everywhere except for the harshest climates in North America and Europe. The berries can be a bit sparse nowadays as summers are getting hotter and drier, but this drink needs only a handful. Go for a bit of a wander, pick a few berries, and you're already halfway done.

½ cup (100 grams) blackberries

2 small sprigs thyme, stems on, plus more for garnish

Zest and juice of ½ lemon

1 teaspoon honey (optional)

2 cups (500 ml) Basic Black Kombucha (page 217)

In a deep container, muddle the blackberries with the thyme, lemon zest and juice, and honey (if using). Split evenly between two glasses and top with kombucha. Garnish with extra thyme and serve immediately.

NOTE

To make this into a cocktail, add half a shot of vodka to each glass before pouring in the kombucha.

A chocolate tart like this one is always my go-to when I need something that pleases a crowd. It's hard to tell that this is vegan, or healthy-ish, or gluten-free, or added sugar-free. Put chocolate in it and I swear no one will notice or care how healthy something is. A chocolate ganache is about as good as it gets for any dessert, and this is no exception. Topping with berries cuts through the richness a bit— as it's very rich indeed.

NOTES

Depending on how much condensation you're willing to risk in your refrigerator, you can pop this on a shelf while the filling is still hot and cool it very quickly, or even freeze for 30 minutes before refrigerating. I've done this, but it's not the best for the health of your appliance!

Hazelnut and almond butter are my favourite options here, but natural peanut butter gives a nice buckeye kind of flavour, too.

Berry Chocolate Tart

Serves eight to ten | 10 minutes prep time | 25 minutes cooking time | 5 to 6 hours cooling and chilling time

Tart Base

1 cup (120 grams) oat flour

½ teaspoon salt

¾ cup (150 grams) Nut and Seed Butter (page 240), or another nut butter

¼ cup (60 ml) maple syrup

2 tablespoons non-dairy milk

1 tablespoon solid coconut oil

1 teaspoon vanilla extract

Chocolate Ganache Filling

3½ ounces (100 grams) dark chocolate, coarsely chopped

1 can (13½ ounces / 400 ml) full-fat coconut milk

½ teaspoon vanilla extract

Pinch salt

Maple syrup, to sweeten (optional)

Toppings

1 batch Whipped Coconut Cream (page 256)

1 cup (200 grams) mixed berries

Dark chocolate, shaved

1 to 2 tablespoons maple syrup (optional)

Preheat the oven to 350°F (180°C) and grease a 9-inch (23 cm) tart tin or springform pan with coconut oil.

To make the base, add the flour, salt, nut and seed butter, maple syrup, milk, coconut oil, and vanilla to a large bowl and mix with a wooden spoon for about 30 seconds, until a stiff dough forms. Use your hands to press the dough into the prepared pan, going about 1½ inches (4 cm) up the side if using a springform.

Use a fork to poke holes in the base and sides of the pastry. Bake for 22 to 25 minutes, or until golden brown. Cool for 10 minutes before removing the sides of the springform pan, then for an additional minimum 30 minutes before pouring in the ganache.

While the tart shell is cooling, prepare the ganache filling. Place the chocolate in a large heatproof bowl. Heat the coconut milk in a small saucepan over medium-low heat until simmering, then pour over the chocolate. Let this rest for one full minute before adding the vanilla and salt and whisking until very smooth. Taste and add maple syrup, if desired.

Pour the ganache into the cooled tart shell, then cool for another 30 minutes at room temperature before refrigerating and cooling fully, about 4 hours.

To serve, top with the whipped cream, berries, chocolate shavings, and maple syrup (if using). Serve chilled.

GF

A bit of a late summer dessert, with plums and the second run of raspberries. As this is a crumble, the queen of easygoing desserts, the size of the dish you use doesn't matter much. A small, deep dish is lovely, as is a standard casserole dish. Mine is 8 inches (20 cm) in diameter, but I often make this in a larger rectangular dish without altering the baking time.

Plum Berry Crumble

Serves four | 10 minutes prep time | 50 minutes cooking time

Fruit Filling

2½ pounds (1 kilogram) plums, pitted and quartered

1 cup (200 grams) raspberries

2 teaspoons maple syrup

1 teaspoon finely grated fresh ginger

Crumble Topping

⅓ cup (80 grams) soft pitted dates

¼ cup (60 grams) solid coconut oil

2 tablespoons non-dairy milk

¾ cup (75 grams) almond flour

¾ cup (75 grams) rolled oats

1 teaspoon cinnamon

Ice cream, for serving (optional)

Preheat the oven to 350°F (180°C).

Place the plums and raspberries in an 8-inch (20 cm) casserole dish. Add the maple syrup and ginger, and mix to coat the fruit.

To make the topping, place the dates, coconut oil, and milk in a food processor and blend until a smooth paste forms. Add the almond flour, oats, and cinnamon and pulse until combined. Crumble the topping in an even layer over the fruit.

Bake for 45 to 50 minutes, or until golden and bubbling. If the topping starts to darken too soon, cover with a lid or baking sheet about halfway through the baking time. Cool for 15 minutes before serving, with ice cream if you have it. This keeps well for up to 3 days in a sealed container, refrigerated.

Peach Melba Ice Cream

Serves six, generously | 10 minutes prep time | 10 minutes cooking time | 30 minutes churning and freezing time

Peach melba was invented in the early 1890s and has largely held onto its popularity, unlike orange omelettes (good riddance). It's vanilla ice cream with raspberries and peaches, but for this version, you're making two quick jams and mixing them into a simple coconut-milk ice cream base instead. The ice cream doesn't need to be cooked and doesn't include eggs, but you do need an ice cream maker for this recipe. If you don't have one, make peach melba popsicles!

Peach Jam

2 peaches, peeled, pitted, and
    chopped

1 tablespoon water

1 tablespoon honey

Raspberry Jam

1 cup (200 grams) raspberries

1 tablespoon water

1 tablespoon honey

Ice Cream Base

1 can (13½ ounces / 400 ml)
    full-fat coconut milk

7 ounces (200 ml) coconut
    cream

3 tablespoons honey

1 teaspoon vanilla extract

To make the peach jam, place the peaches, water, and honey in a small saucepan and simmer over medium-low heat for about 10 minutes, stirring frequently. It should be thickened and jam-like when finished. Set aside to cool.

While the peach jam is simmering, make the raspberry jam. Place the raspberries, water, and honey in a small saucepan and simmer over medium-low heat for 5 minutes. It doesn't thicken as much as the peach jam, and should be almost compote-like in consistency. Mash the berries if needed, and set aside to cool.

Split the peach jam into two equal parts, setting one half aside. To make the ice cream, whisk the coconut milk, coconut cream, honey, vanilla, and half of the peach jam together in a large bowl until combined. Churn, following the instructions for your ice cream maker, until creamy.

Scoop the ice cream into a large container (at least 4 cups / 1 litre), like a silicone or parchment-lined bread tin, and drizzle the cooled raspberry jam and the remaining peach jam over it. Use a spoon or skewer to swirl in the jams for a rippled effect. Freeze for 10 minutes before serving.

To store this ice cream, simply freeze in a sealed container. Thaw for 10 to 15 minutes at room temperature before serving if frozen solid.

NOTE

To make popsicles, add the three elements in spoonfuls, starting with the ice cream base, to popsicle moulds and use a skewer or butter knife to swirl together. Add popsicle sticks or metal spoons to each popsicle and freeze until solid.

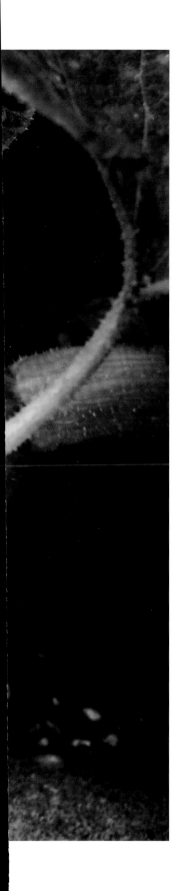

Autumn

Harvest, overabundance, shorter days, and cooler nights. Autumn is bittersweet. I like this time of year—I like foraging, picking mushrooms and elderberries, fresh apples, the return to baking—but I don't like that winter is around the corner and that I start to feel those lower light levels. So take it day by day and forget that winter will be here soon; it's a beautiful time of year. There is a true plethora of produce.

Autumn is comfort food to a tee, with pumpkin, apples, and spices galore set on a backdrop of changing leaves and end-of-season bonfires. It's a romantic time. In Manitoba, where the seasons move so suddenly, it's a very lucky thing if the leaves change before they fall. Here in northern Europe, the season moves slowly and there's a mix of blackberries, mushrooms, root veg, winter squash, and hardier herbs.

This is the largest chapter in this book, reflecting the quantity of fruits and vegetables, nuts, and seeds available, a return to holiday gatherings, and more time spent indoors. A couple of recipes in this chapter work very well for a plant-based holiday meal, particularly the filled pumpkins and rosemary roasted roots. I included an ice cream cake, more because the flavour profile is more appropriate for this season than because we necessarily want frozen food in autumn, but it is very good even on a cool day. And although I wanted to include some kind of bread in every season, I had to restrain myself, so this is the only one with cinnamon rolls.

I think this is truly the best time of year for cooks and bakers. There's so much to enjoy, and though that's the case in every season, there seems to be more time and the desire to use what's available in autumn. Turn that oven on and embrace this season while it lasts.

GF | NF | SF

Root Veg Fritters

Makes about twelve fritters | 10 minutes prep time |
10 minutes cooking time

I grew up on latkes, often with extra veggies mixed in, and they were a speedy dinnertime favourite for my mom. I like them most in the morning, but of course you can also have them for lunch or as a light dinner. Latkes should be eaten with applesauce, but I can't shake my love of ketchup—though not with this version, of course, which is best with a dollop of bean dip, hummus, or apple butter instead.

1 medium beet

1 medium carrot

1 medium potato

1 small onion

2 tablespoons thyme leaves

¼ cup (30 grams) chickpea flour

2 tablespoons olive oil, plus more for frying

2 tablespoons water

1 tablespoon apple cider vinegar

½ teaspoon salt

½ teaspoon freshly ground pepper

¼ teaspoon cayenne pepper

Thyme Roasted Garlic Bean Dip (page 128), Apple Jalapeño Butter (page 131), or Caramelized Onion Hummus (page 181), for serving

Coarsely grate the beet, carrot, potato, and onion into a large bowl, using a standard box grater or a food processor to make quick work of it. You want about 1½ cups (300 grams) of grated vegetables altogether.

Stir the thyme, chickpea flour, oil, water, vinegar, salt, pepper, and cayenne into the bowl and mix well.

Heat a large frying pan over medium heat and add a generous drizzle of olive oil. Drop 2 tablespoons of the vegetable mixture into the hot pan for each fritter. Cook for about 3 minutes, flip, flatten with a spatula, and cook for an additional 3 minutes. Repeat until all the batter has been used, placing the cooked fritters in a warm oven (about 120°F / 50°C) while you continue cooking.

Serve the fritters hot with some roasted garlic bean dip, apple jalapeño butter, or hummus. They're best eaten fresh, but can be refrigerated for a couple of days in an airtight container and reheated in a frying pan.

Apple Hazelnut Waffles

Serves two to four | 5 minutes prep time | 10 minutes cooking time

Waffles are infinitely better than pancakes, no arguments accepted. Crispy outside, fluffy inside, what's not to like? Hazelnut meal adds a little richness to this recipe, while olive oil and apple provide a bit of depth. If you're making these for kids, you can sub a lighter-tasting oil instead, like grapeseed, but the olive oil is quite subtle. This makes six waffles for me in my Belgian-style waffle iron.

1½ cups (225 grams) spelt flour

½ cup (50 grams) hazelnut meal

2 tablespoons coconut sugar

1 tablespoon arrowroot powder

1½ teaspoons baking powder

1 teaspoon cinnamon

½ teaspoon baking soda

½ teaspoon salt

½ teaspoon freshly ground nutmeg

1 teaspoon apple cider vinegar

1¼ cups (300 ml) non-dairy milk

¼ cup (60 ml) olive oil

1 large apple, shredded

Maple syrup, for serving

Preheat your waffle iron on medium-high while you prepare the batter.

Add the flour, hazelnut meal, sugar, arrowroot powder, baking powder, cinnamon, baking soda, salt, and nutmeg to a large bowl. Stir the apple cider vinegar into the milk, then add this mixture to the bowl, along with the oil and apple. Stir until just combined.

Fill each well in the waffle iron about three-quarters full. Bake the waffles in the hot iron, about 5 minutes each depending on the type of waffle iron you're using. They should be golden brown, with a crisp exterior. To keep the finished waffles warm while baking the next batch, place them on the rack of a warm (not hot, maybe 120°F / 50°C) oven. Serve warm with maple syrup.

NOTES

You can make your own hazelnut meal by blending raw hazelnuts at high speed in a food processor for a few minutes, or until a fine meal has formed but before any oil releases from the nuts. If you blend too long, you'll start to make hazelnut butter (also good).

I never peel apples, and especially not when shredding them for a recipe. You won't notice the skin.

GF | NF | SF | YR

Chocolate Sunflower Seed Bites

Makes about twenty bites | 10 minutes prep time

This is my base recipe for snack bites and what I stick to most of the time, sometimes adding in pricier elements. Sunflower seeds are cheap, neutral tasting, and packed with good stuff. A handful of walnuts or hazelnuts subbed for some of the seeds is nice, as is using hazelnut oil instead of coconut. These bites are quite flexible and easy to make year-round.

¾ cup (105 grams) sunflower seeds

½ cup (120 grams) soft pitted dates

2 tablespoons cacao powder, plus more for rolling

1 tablespoon solid coconut oil

½ teaspoon cinnamon

½ teaspoon vanilla extract

Pinch salt

Blend the sunflower seeds in a food processor until a coarse meal forms. Add the dates, cacao powder, coconut oil, cinnamon, vanilla, and salt and blend until a ball of dough forms, adding a splash of water to help it along if your dates are on the hard side.

Roll the dough into small balls, about a tablespoon each. Roll the bites in cacao powder (optional) and refrigerate or freeze in a sealed container. They keep well, refrigerated, for up to 2 weeks.

GF

My first job was in an ice cream shop, and maple walnut was one of the most popular flavours. You might think it was only elderly people who got it, but little kids loved it too, probably because it's so overwhelmingly sweet. This granola, though inspired by those flavours, edges on savoury with its small amount of syrup and slightly bitter walnuts. If you like your granola to be just mildly sweet, very far off from the store-bought kind, this is it.

Maple Walnut Granola

Makes about 4 cups (450 grams) | 5 minutes prep time | 35 minutes cooking time

2 cups (220 grams) rolled oats

1 cup (150 grams) coarsely chopped raw walnuts

¼ cup (50 grams) chia seeds

2 teaspoons cinnamon

½ teaspoon freshly ground nutmeg

¼ teaspoon salt

¼ cup (60 ml) melted coconut oil

¼ cup (60 ml) maple syrup

Preheat the oven to 300°F (150°C) and line a large baking sheet with parchment paper.

In a large bowl, stir together the oats, walnuts, chia, cinnamon, nutmeg, and salt. Add the coconut oil and maple syrup to the dry ingredients and use your hands to mix thoroughly, until fully coated.

Transfer the granola to the baking sheet, wet your hands slightly, and use them to spread the granola into a roughly even layer.

Bake for 30 to 35 minutes, or until golden. Remove from the oven and cool fully on the pan (it will become crisper as it cools) before breaking the granola into pieces. Store in a sealed container for up to 1 week at room temperature or 1 month in the refrigerator.

GF | NF

Blackberry Apple Crumble Bars

Makes sixteen small bars | 10 minutes prep time |
30 minutes cooking time

*Pairing foods that grow within
the same season not only is
practical but always tastes better,
too. Blackberries and apples are a
perfect example. These simple
bars do triple duty—breakfast,
snack, or a lighter dessert.*

Crumble Dough

2 cups (220 grams) rolled oats

¼ cup (25 grams) coconut sugar

¼ cup (60 grams) soft pitted
  dates

3 tablespoons solid coconut oil

2 tablespoons non-dairy milk

1 teaspoon vanilla extract

1 teaspoon cinnamon

¼ teaspoon freshly ground
  nutmeg

¼ teaspoon salt

Fruit Filling

2 medium apples (about
  10½ ounces / 300 grams),
  finely chopped

1 cup (200 grams)
  blackberries, lightly mashed
  with a fork

2 tablespoons maple syrup

Juice of ½ lemon

Preheat the oven to 350°F (180°C) and line an 8-inch (20 cm) square
baking tin with parchment paper.

Place the oats in a food processor and blend into a coarse flour. Add
the sugar, dates, oil, milk, vanilla, cinnamon, nutmeg, and salt and
blend until the dates have broken down and a soft, crumbly dough
has formed.

To make the filling, mix the apples, blackberries, maple syrup, and
lemon juice in a bowl and set aside.

Take two-thirds of the crumble dough and press into an even layer in
the baking tin. Top with the blackberry and apple filling, then crumble
the remaining dough over the fruit.

Bake for 25 to 30 minutes, or until golden brown and the fruit is
softened. Cool for 15 minutes before removing from the tin and
cooling fully before slicing into small squares. These will keep well at
room temperature for a few days in an airtight container, and can be
frozen for up to a month.

Sesame Roasted Delicata Squash

Serves four | 10 minutes prep time | 25 minutes cooking time

A neat thing about delicata squash is that, like Hokkaido (red kuri), it doesn't need to be peeled. So although there's some extra work in this recipe to remove the seeds from the slices, it's balanced by not having to peel the squash. Sesame and honey are a great combination, especially with the ginger and lemon here. Try this as a pretty side dish for a holiday get-together or as part of a grain salad.

4 medium delicata squash

1 tablespoon finely grated fresh ginger

2 cloves garlic, finely grated

Zest of 1 lemon

2 tablespoons olive oil

1 tablespoon honey, plus more for serving

1 tablespoon water

½ teaspoon salt

½ teaspoon freshly ground pepper

¼ teaspoon cayenne pepper

½ cup (70 grams) sesame seeds

Preheat the oven to 375°F (190°C) and line a baking sheet with parchment paper.

Cut the delicata squash into ¾-inch (2 cm) rounds. Remove the seeds (see note).

In a large, shallow dish, whisk together the ginger, garlic, lemon zest, oil, honey, water, salt, pepper, and cayenne. Place the sesame seeds in a separate small dish.

Drop the squash slices into the ginger sauce and mix to coat. Use the fork to lift a coated slice, then press one side into the sesame seeds. Place seed side up on the baking sheet and repeat with the other slices.

Bake for 20 to 25 minutes, or until the squash is cooked through and the seeds are golden. Serve hot, with a drizzle of honey.

NOTES

If you can't find delicata, another type of pumpkin cut into small wedges will do just as well, or the slim neck of a butternut, peeled, sliced, and with a hole cut into the centre of each circle.

If you want to avoid removing the seeds from the rounds, you can do half-rounds, seeding after cutting the squash lengthwise. It's not as pretty, but easier if you're pressed for time.

GF

I have a secret to share with you. With the exception of cashews, which are perfect in every way, I hate all raw nuts—it's something about the texture. They are, however, excellent roasted on a chilly autumn day, especially with an abundance of spices and a good dash of maple syrup. Hazelnuts are readily available and inexpensive in autumn, and this is one of the simplest and best ways to enjoy them.

Spicy Roasted Hazelnuts

Makes about 3 cups (500 grams) | 5 minutes prep time | 15 minutes cooking time

3 cups (450 grams) raw hazelnuts

1 tablespoon grapeseed oil

¼ cup (60 ml) maple syrup

2 teaspoons salt

1 teaspoon cinnamon

½ teaspoon cayenne pepper

½ teaspoon ground cumin

½ teaspoon ground coriander

½ teaspoon freshly ground pepper

Preheat the oven to 400°F (200°C) and line a large baking sheet with parchment paper.

Add the hazelnuts to the pan, then drizzle with the oil and maple syrup and sprinkle with the salt, cinnamon, cayenne, cumin, coriander, and pepper. Stir to coat the hazelnuts.

Bake for 12 to 14 minutes, or until golden. Cool fully on the pan before serving or storing. These keep well in a sealed container for up to 1 week.

GF | NF | SF

Rosemary Roasted Roots

Serves four to six | 10 minutes prep time | 1 hour cooking time

Brilliantly simple, this recipe makes excellent use of hardy root vegetables readily available from September right up until winter. A bit of rosemary and vinegar go a long way for this dish, turning humble carrots, parsnips, and beets into something you'll truly enjoy eating. It makes a great meal with a couple poached eggs or with some chickpeas tossed into the pan with the veg.

4 medium carrots, cut into 1-inch (2.5 cm) slices

4 medium parsnips, peeled and cut into 1-inch (2.5 cm) slices

3 small beets, cut into small wedges

2 small onions, peeled and halved

1 head garlic, halved horizontally

2 sprigs rosemary, leaves minced

2 tablespoons white wine vinegar

2 tablespoons olive oil

1 teaspoon salt

1 teaspoon freshly ground pepper

Preheat the oven to 375°F (190°C).

Place the carrots, parsnips, beets, onions, garlic, rosemary, vinegar, oil, salt, and pepper in a large casserole dish or deep-sided pan and stir to combine. Roast for 50 to 60 minutes, or until the vegetables are fork-tender. Serve hot. Leftovers can be kept in the refrigerator for a couple of days in a sealed container.

GF | NF | SF

Thyme Roasted Garlic Bean Dip

Makes about 2 cups (425 grams) | 5 minutes prep time

White beans make for a very creamy, silky smooth dip, and roasted garlic adds a mellow sweetness, making this a good choice to bring to work or school without worrying about estranging your coworkers. Try this with the Meso Bowl (page 140) or Moroccan Aubergines (page 143), or serve it with crackers or veg, as a bread spread, or any way you might usually use hummus.

1½ cups (225 grams) cooked or canned white beans, drained and rinsed

3 cloves Roasted Garlic (page 251)

½ teaspoon salt

½ teaspoon freshly ground pepper

¼ teaspoon cayenne pepper

2 tablespoons thyme leaves, plus more for serving

Juice of 1 lemon

3 tablespoons olive oil, plus more for serving

Add the beans, garlic, salt, pepper, cayenne, thyme, and lemon juice to a food processor or blender and mix well. Pour in the oil in a slow stream, blending on low speed, until the dip is very smooth and velvety. Serve immediately, topped with more olive oil and thyme, or refrigerate for up to a week.

GF | NF

Apple Jalapeño Butter

Makes about 1½ cups (375 ml) | 10 minutes prep time |
1 hour cooking time

Apple butter is a special treat. I used to make it every year with the crabapples from my childhood home (sour apples make excellent apple butter, so you know), and the coring, cutting, and cooking can be a meditative process. This version is a bit spicy and has a more layered flavour than regular apple butter. Think of this much as you would a chutney, rather than a sweet spread, and serve it with latkes, with bean burgers, or as part of a mezze.

2½ pounds (1 kilogram) apples, cored and diced

2 tablespoons water

Juice of 1 lemon

2 tablespoons honey

1 jalapeño pepper, minced

1 teaspoon minced fresh ginger

1 teaspoon cinnamon

Add the apples and water to a large saucepan. Bring to a low boil over medium heat, then reduce and simmer, covered, for about 30 minutes. The apples should be very soft.

Purée the apples with an immersion blender. You can use a heat-safe blender too; just return the puréed apples to the pan. Add the lemon juice, honey, jalapeño, ginger, and cinnamon.

Gently simmer over low heat, uncovered, stirring frequently. After 30 minutes it should be significantly thickened and darker in colour.

Spoon the apple butter into heat-safe jars, or cool before placing into containers. It lasts up to 2 weeks in the refrigerator. I have canned this recipe before, but recommend freezing it instead if you want to hold onto it longer. To freeze, simply fill jars or airtight containers, leaving some space at the top for expansion. It'll last up to 3 months in the freezer.

NOTES

To reduce the spice level, remove the seeds from the jalapeño before adding to the puréed apples.

Speed up this recipe by using premade applesauce instead of cooking and puréeing the apples yourself.

GF | NF | SF

Green Cauliflower Soup

Serves four | 10 minutes prep time | 20 minutes cooking time

A good soup is always worthwhile, but invaluable in a vegetable-centric diet, and even more so in a budget-friendly one. A blended soup like this one is a great way to use up some veggies on their last legs. Ginger, cayenne pepper, and a squeeze of lemon add a bit of heat and freshness to an otherwise simple dish. Frozen cauliflower can easily be used instead of fresh for this soup, and the beans blend seamlessly to add a touch of creaminess to this uncomplicated meal.

1 teaspoon olive oil

1 small onion, diced

3 cloves garlic, minced

1 tablespoon finely grated fresh ginger

1 teaspoon salt

1 teaspoon freshly ground pepper

¼ teaspoon cayenne pepper

1 head cauliflower, cut into small florets

4 cups (1 litre) Vegetable Stock (page 243)

2 cups (300 grams) cooked or canned chickpeas or white beans, drained and rinsed

3 cups (70 grams) chopped Swiss chard (see note)

Juice of 1 lemon

Heat a large pot over medium-low heat. Add the olive oil, followed by the onions. Sauté for 3 minutes, until the onions are translucent, then add the garlic and ginger and cook for another minute. Stir in the salt, pepper, cayenne, and cauliflower and cook for about 30 seconds more. Pour in the stock and bring to a boil, covered, over high heat.

Add the chickpeas and reduce to a low simmer. Cook, covered, for another 15 minutes, stirring occasionally, then remove from the heat and stir in the Swiss chard. Purée with an immersion blender or carefully in a heat-safe standing blender. Add the lemon juice and season if necessary. Serve hot. Leftovers can be refrigerated in a sealed container for up to 3 days or frozen for up to a month.

NOTE
Any type of hardy green (kale, spinach, arugula) can be substituted for the chard in this recipe. Frozen also works.

NF | SF

Golden Pumpkin and Chickpea Stew

Serves four | 10 minutes prep time | 40 minutes cooking time

Pumpkin stew is a must-have in autumn, and you can't go wrong with a curry-inspired, coconut-scented broth. There's no better comfort food than a good stew, and the warming spices featured here make this a particularly good one. When I'm feeling poorly from the changing season and lower light levels, this is one of the recipes I always turn to—both the taste and colour are guaranteed to cheer you up.

2 teaspoons coconut oil

1 small yellow onion, diced

1 small pumpkin, cut into 1-inch (2.5 cm) pieces (see note)

3 cloves garlic, minced

1 teaspoon finely grated fresh ginger

1 teaspoon salt

½ teaspoon ground turmeric

½ teaspoon ground cumin

½ teaspoon ground coriander

½ teaspoon freshly ground pepper

¼ teaspoon cinnamon

1 tablespoon apple cider vinegar

1 can (13½ ounces / 400 grams) diced tomatoes

1 can (13½ ounces / 400 ml) full-fat coconut milk

1 cup (250 ml) Vegetable Stock (page 243)

2 cups (300 grams) cooked or canned chickpeas, drained and rinsed

3 cups (70 grams) chopped or baby spinach

Garlic Spelt Naan (page 178) or brown rice, for serving

Chopped cilantro or parsley, for serving

NOTES

Hokkaido is my favourite pumpkin variety to use in soups and stews as it doesn't need to be peeled. If you use a different type of pumpkin or winter squash, make sure to peel it before chopping.

Substitute 2 teaspoons of the Curry Spice Blend (page 248) for the individual spices in this recipe if you're short on time.

Heat the coconut oil in a large pot over medium heat. Add the onions and cook for 2 to 3 minutes, until softened and fragrant. Stir in the pumpkin and cook for another 5 minutes, stirring frequently.

Add the garlic, ginger, salt, turmeric, cumin, coriander, pepper, and cinnamon and cook for another minute, stirring. Pour in the vinegar, followed by the tomatoes, coconut milk, and stock.

Bring to a low boil, then add the chickpeas. Reduce the heat and simmer for about 30 minutes, or until the pumpkin is fork-tender.

Taste and season as necessary, then remove from the heat and stir in the spinach. Serve hot with naan or brown rice, topped with cilantro or parsley. Leftovers keep very well, refrigerated in a sealed container, for up to 4 days.

GF | SF

Smoky Mushroom Pumpkin Chili

Serves six to eight | 15 minutes prep time | 30 minutes cooking time

Chili is a vegetarian mainstay, and the seared mushrooms here give the best meaty texture, alongside a toasted flavour and slight crunch from the walnuts. A vegan chili without these types of additions is a sad one indeed, as it falls flat without extras to add depth and interest to the dish. This is a bit of an early autumn meal, blending both corn and pumpkin.

NOTES

The vegetables can sometimes stick to the pot during the first two steps, especially with aluminum pots. The vinegar and tomatoes should lift any stuck bits when they're added, and they improve the flavour of the chili.

To toast the nuts, add them to a dry frying pan over medium-low heat and stir regularly for about 5 minutes, or until the oils start to release and the nuts are browned.

Any type of winter squash can be used in this recipe. I recommend Hokkaido, butternut, or Sugar Pie. If not using Hokkaido, make sure to peel it before chopping.

1 tablespoon olive oil

3 cups (300 grams) chopped button mushrooms

1 large onion, diced

1 small pumpkin (1 pound / 500 grams), cut into 1-inch (2.5 cm) pieces (see note)

3 cloves garlic, minced

1 teaspoon cumin seeds

1 teaspoon salt

1 teaspoon smoked paprika

½ teaspoon freshly ground pepper

½ teaspoon cayenne pepper

½ teaspoon cinnamon

1 tablespoon apple cider vinegar

1 can (13½ ounces / 400 grams) diced tomatoes

2 cups (500 ml) Vegetable Stock (page 243)

½ cup (90 grams) dry quinoa

1½ cups (225 grams) cooked or canned kidney beans

1 cup (150 grams) fresh or frozen corn

3 cups (70 grams) chopped Swiss chard

½ cup (75 grams) coarsely chopped walnuts, toasted

2 to 3 green onions, chopped, for serving

Coconut Yogurt (page 228), for serving

Heat the oil in a large pot over medium heat. Make sure the pan is very hot before adding the mushrooms, then sear until the mushrooms are golden brown and any water has evaporated, about 5 minutes, stirring once halfway through. This might take longer if the mushrooms have a high water content.

Add the onions and pumpkin and cook for another 5 minutes, stirring frequently, until softened. Stir in the garlic, cumin, salt, paprika, pepper, cayenne, and cinnamon, cooking briefly, then add the vinegar. Pour in the tomatoes and stock.

Bring to a rolling boil, add the quinoa, then reduce to a simmer. Cook, covered, for another 10 minutes.

Once the quinoa is cooked through, stir in the beans and corn. Turn off the heat, add the chard and walnuts, and cover to wilt the greens. Season as needed and serve hot with green onions and a spoonful of yogurt.

GF

Chickpea Waldorf Salad

Serves two to four | 10 minutes prep time | 30 minutes cooking time

Waldorf salad is an old recipe, originally from 1896, and has remained popular for well over a century. It's traditionally made with mayonnaise, but yogurt lightens things up in this version. Apple and celery add crunch to this protein-packed salad, grapes add sweetness, and chickpeas, walnuts, and a very non-traditional coconut yogurt dressing round it out. It may be inspired by a century-old recipe, but it's anything but old-fashioned.

Salad

13½ ounces (400 grams) seedless grapes

2 cloves garlic, skin on

½ teaspoon olive oil

¼ teaspoon salt

¼ teaspoon freshly ground pepper

½ teaspoon sumac

2 cups (300 grams) cooked or canned chickpeas, drained and rinsed

1 large apple, sliced

3 stalks celery, cut in ¾-inch (2 cm) diagonal slices

½ cup (75 grams) raw walnuts

Yogurt Dressing

¼ cup (60 ml) Coconut Yogurt (page 228, see note)

Zest of 1 lemon

Juice of 1 lemon

½ teaspoon Dijon mustard

½ teaspoon maple syrup

½ teaspoon salt

½ teaspoon freshly ground pepper

Water if needed, to thin

NOTES

If you don't want to have a very mild coconut flavour here, sub in a large ripe avocado for the yogurt.

If you want to speed up the process, skip roasting the grapes. Roasting concentrates the flavour and there's plenty of crunch remaining with the apple and celery, but it does add a half hour in the oven, and the salad is excellent either way.

Preheat the oven to 400°F (200°C) and line a baking sheet with parchment paper.

Place the grapes and garlic on the baking sheet and gently mix with the oil, salt, pepper, and sumac. Roast for 25 to 30 minutes, or until softened and dark purple (or yellow, for green grapes).

While the grapes are roasting, prepare the dressing. Whisk the yogurt, lemon zest, lemon juice, mustard, maple syrup, salt, and pepper in a small bowl until well mixed, and set aside. If the dressing is too thick to pour, add a touch of water to thin as needed.

In a large bowl, mix the chickpeas, apples, celery, and walnuts. Stir in the yogurt dressing. Serve the salad on a large plate or platter topped with the roasted grapes. (If you want to use fresh grapes, simply mix them in with the other ingredients instead.) Leftovers keep well in a sealed container in the refrigerator for up to 3 days.

GF | NF | SF

Meso Bowl

Serves two | 10 minutes prep time | 30 minutes cooking time

Meso is shortened from "Mesoamerican," a historical/ anthropological term referring to a cultural region centred in what's now modern-day Mexico and Central America. My first thought was the Three Sisters—a traditional way to grow squash, beans, and corn—for this one, but I chose sweet potato to highlight another great autumn vegetable instead. Either way, these ingredients are excellent together and this is a phenomenal weeknight dinner. Sweet potato and rice make up the base for this zesty dish, brightened up with pickled onions, spicy arugula, and lime. Easy, healthy, filling— the trifecta of the perfect meal.

1 medium sweet potato, cut into ½-inch (1 cm) rounds

1 teaspoon olive oil

½ teaspoon salt

½ teaspoon freshly ground pepper

1 cup (200 grams) cooked brown rice (see page 11)

¼ cup (15 grams) chopped oregano

2 handfuls arugula

¼ cup (60 grams) Pickled Red Onions (page 254)

¼ cup (60 grams) Thyme Roasted Garlic Bean Dip (page 128)

Juice of 1 lime

Spicy Black Beans

2 teaspoons olive oil

1 small red onion, diced

2 cloves garlic, minced

½ teaspoon cumin seeds

¼ teaspoon cayenne pepper

¼ teaspoon salt

¼ teaspoon freshly ground pepper

1½ cups (225 grams) cooked or canned black beans, drained and rinsed

1 tablespoon lime juice

Preheat the oven to 375°F (190°C). Place the sweet potatoes on a baking sheet and use your hands to coat with the olive oil, salt, and pepper. Bake for 20 to 25 minutes, or until lightly browned.

While the sweet potatoes are cooking, cook the rice if it hasn't been cooked ahead of time, then stir the oregano into it.

To make the spicy black beans, heat the oil in a large pan over medium heat. Add the onions and sauté for 4 to 5 minutes, or until softened and translucent. Stir in the garlic, cumin, cayenne, salt, and pepper. Cook for another minute before adding the beans and lime juice. Lower the heat and cook for a couple more minutes to heat the beans. Cover and set aside.

To assemble, split everything between two bowls. Layer the rice, sweet potatoes, arugula, and then black beans, then top with the pickled onions, bean dip, and finally lime juice. Serve hot. Leftovers keep well in the refrigerator for a couple of days and are excellent at room temperature. This makes a good work lunch.

NF | SF

Moroccan Aubergines

Serves four | 10 minutes prep time | 20 minutes cooking time

I tried a dish similar to this one at a local vegan restaurant, and the battered eggplant was so enjoyable, with a texture that's not often found in plant-based cooking. Chickpea flour is very eggy and gives a nice coating that's both crisp and soft, and really makes the dish into more of a meal. The aubergine (eggplant) becomes very soft, almost buttery, with a spicy battered outer layer that makes these absolutely addictive.

1 cup (120 grams) chickpea flour

3 tablespoons arrowroot powder

1½ teaspoons baking powder

2 teaspoons Moroccan Spice Blend (page 248)

½ teaspoon salt

¾ cup (180 ml) warm water

2 tablespoons olive oil

1 teaspoon apple cider vinegar

Coconut oil, for frying

2 medium eggplants, sliced into ¾-inch (2 cm) slices

To Serve

Thyme Roasted Garlic Bean Dip (page 128) or Caramelized Onion Hummus (page 181)

Garlic Spelt Naan (page 178)

Chermoula (page 244)

In a shallow bowl, whisk together the chickpea flour, arrowroot powder, baking powder, spice blend, and salt. Stir in the water, olive oil, and vinegar, mixing until no lumps remain.

Heat a large frying pan over medium heat and add enough coconut oil to just cover the base of the pan. Use the largest frying pan you have, or use two, to try to get as many rounds fried at once as you can.

Once the pan is hot, dip the eggplant slices into the chickpea flour batter and fry for 1 to 2 minutes each side, until crisp and golden. Repeat until all of the eggplant is fried.

Serve hot with bean dip (or hummus), naan, and chermoula.

NOTES

Alternatively, the battered eggplant rounds can be baked at 400°F (200°C) for 30 to 35 minutes, but they are better fried.

I recommend coconut oil when frying because olive oil tends to splatter.

Savoury Autumn Farinata

Serves two to four | 10 minutes prep time | 1 hour resting time | 35 minutes cooking time

Farinata, or socca, is a type of flatbread made with chickpea flour and a great low-effort dinner. I think it can be so nice to have a filling vegetarian dinner that doesn't include obvious legumes sometimes. This version relies on fresh thyme, meaty mushrooms, and sweet apples for a quintessentially autumn meal. Apple and mushroom are great together; if you're skeptical, just try it.

Farinata Batter

1 cup (120 grams) chickpea flour

1 cup (250 ml) water

2 tablespoons olive oil

2 cloves garlic, minced

1 tablespoon thyme leaves

1 teaspoon freshly ground pepper

½ teaspoon salt

1 tablespoon solid coconut oil

2 cups (200 grams) button mushrooms, sliced

1 small onion, thinly sliced

½ teaspoon salt

½ teaspoon freshly ground pepper

1 small apple, thinly sliced

Basic Tahini Dressing (page 247), for topping

Arugula or baby spinach, for serving

At least 1 hour before you're ready to bake, make the farinata batter. Whisk the flour, water, olive oil, garlic, thyme, pepper, and salt in a large bowl until no visible lumps remain, and cover. Leave it out at room temperature to rest for 1 hour. The batter can be refrigerated for up to 12 hours before use (see note) and should rest in the refrigerator if you mix it 2 or more hours before cooking.

Place the coconut oil, mushrooms, onions, salt, and pepper in an 8-inch (20 cm) cast-iron pan. Place the pan in the oven and heat to 400°F (200°C) (see note).

Once the oven is heated, check on the vegetables. If there's still water in the pan from the mushrooms, bake for another 5 to 10 minutes.

Once all the water is evaporated, pour the batter over the vegetables in the hot pan and scatter the apple slices over top. Bake for 22 to 25 minutes, or until golden. Serve plain or with tahini dressing and arugula or spinach. Farinata tends to dry out a bit when stored and is best eaten fresh, but it will last a day or two in a sealed container at room temperature.

NOTES

Try mixing the batter and popping it in the refrigerator before leaving the house in the morning. It'll be ready when you're back in the evening, for a quick and easy dinner.

The vegetables are partially roasted while the pan heats up, before the batter is added, drawing most of the water out of the mushrooms.

Show-Stopping Moroccan Stuffed Pumpkin

Serves four to six | 20 minutes prep time | 1 hour cooking time

A true centrepiece main filled with autumn goodness—sage, walnuts, apple—all tied together with a healthy dose of Moroccan flavours. If you're having people over for autumn holidays or get-togethers, this is one vegan option that won't look sad next to a turkey. And I promise, any vegetarians will be thrilled not to have to live off salad and mashed potatoes!

1 large pumpkin (about 5 pounds / 2 kilograms, see note)

4 tablespoons olive oil, divided

1 cup (220 grams) dry bulgur

1½ cups (375 ml) water

1 teaspoon salt, plus a pinch more, divided

Pinch saffron (optional)

4 sage leaves

1 red onion, chopped

½ cup (75 grams) coarsely chopped raw walnuts

3 cloves garlic, minced

1 teaspoon Moroccan Spice Blend (page 248)

1 teaspoon freshly ground pepper

1 cup (150 grams) cooked or canned white beans, drained and rinsed

1 medium apple, shredded

¼ cup (40 grams) raisins

To Serve

Basic Tahini Dressing (page 247)

½ cup (50 grams) pomegranate arils

2 tablespoons finely chopped mint leaves

Preheat the oven to 375°F (190°C).

Cut the top of the pumpkin out, making a hole large enough for your hand. Cut on a slight inward angle so that the top can sit in the pumpkin like a lid. Remove the seeds and brush 3 tablespoons oil over the inner cavity of the pumpkin. Replace the top and bake for 40 to 45 minutes. When done, it should be fairly easy to pierce with a sharp knife, but it shouldn't fall apart. The outside will be darkened. Keep the oven on for the second bake.

While the pumpkin is cooking, prepare the bulgur. Place the bulgur, water, pinch of salt, and saffron (if using) in a small saucepan over high heat. Bring to a boil, then reduce and simmer, covered, for 10 minutes. Set aside.

Heat a large frying pan over medium heat. Add the remaining 1 table-spoon oil. Fry the sage in the hot pan for 1 to 2 minutes, or until very crispy. Place on a kitchen towel and set aside.

recipe continues . . .

Add the onions and walnuts to the pan and cook, stirring frequently, for 5 minutes. Stir in the garlic, spice blend, the remaining 1 teaspoon salt, and pepper and cook for another 30 seconds or so.

Break the sage into pieces and add it with the onion mixture to the cooked bulgur. Stir in the beans, apple, and raisins. Stuff the pre-baked pumpkin with this mixture (see note) and bake for another 15 to 20 minutes.

To serve, cut the pumpkin into wedges and serve each with the filling and a drizzle of tahini dressing, pomegranate arils, and mint.

NOTES

Any type of pumpkin you love can be used here. With Hokkaido you can also eat the skin, which is great, but I love Musquee, Cinderella, or Blue Hubbard. Butternut doesn't give the large internal cavity required for this recipe—you'll need the classic pumpkin shape.

To make this gluten-free, substitute rice for the bulgur, and for a nut-free option, use sunflower or pumpkin seeds in place of walnuts.

The pumpkin doesn't need to cool before stuffing, but don't worry if it's ready before the other elements are. It'll heat through during the second bake.

Although the cooking time seems very involved, everything is finished within an hour, since you prep the filling while the pumpkin is having its first bake. You can also make everything the day before and simply heat through before serving.

GF | NF | YR

Honey Halva Latte

Serves two | 5 minutes prep time | 5 minutes cooking time

Despite my older sister's best efforts, I never got into coffee, and always ordered sweet steamed milk at coffee shops. This is a less sweet, more adult-appropriate version of that treat. Slightly bitter tahini is a counterpoint to the honey, with a bit of spice for a very cozy drink. I like to use a blend of cream mixed with milk for this recipe, either store-bought oat or homemade cashew depending on how luxurious I'm feeling that day. Oat wins 99 percent of the time (but cashew is better).

2 cups (500 ml) non-dairy milk

2 teaspoons tahini

½ teaspoon cinnamon

½ teaspoon vanilla extract

Tiny pinch salt

1 tablespoon honey

Nutmeg, grated, for topping

Mix the milk, tahini, cinnamon, vanilla, and salt into a small saucepan and heat over medium-low heat, until simmering. Cook for a couple of minutes, then remove from the heat, stir in honey, and use an immersion blender to mix on high speed until foaming. Serve in mugs, topped with the milk foam and a pinch of grated nutmeg.

Autumn Abundance Tea

Makes just over 1 cup (200 grams) loose tea | 10 minutes prep time |
3 to 4 days drying time

*This tea is a version of my
favourite autumn fruit tea that's
very common in Germany. I drink
a big pot of it every morning as I
start work and often throughout
the day when it's cold outside—it's
a great way to get more liquids in
without added sugar, and it tastes
great. Like the Winter Spice Tea
(page 203), this makes a beautiful
gift, and it's nice and mild.*

2 large apples, cut into ¾-inch (2 cm) pieces

1 teaspoon lemon juice

½ cup (120 grams) rosehips

1 thumb ginger (about 3 inches / 8 cm), julienned

2 cinnamon sticks, broken into pieces

¼ cup (40 grams) raisins

¼ cup (40 grams) almonds, chopped

2 tablespoons calendula petals

Mix the apples and lemon juice in a bowl to coat the fruit. This helps
reduce browning.

Dry the apples, rosehips, and ginger on a large tea towel in a dry and,
if possible, sunny spot. They should be completely dry to the touch
when ready, after 3 to 4 days. Mix these dried ingredients with the
cinnamon sticks, raisins, almonds, and calendula petals, and package
in a paper bag. Use within 3 months.

To brew the tea, steep 2 tablespoons of tea in a cup of boiling water for
5 to 8 minutes.

NOTE

*Rosehips can be found in many wooded areas in autumn, or from a garden,
or can be purchased online.*

*Calendula is a great plant to grow in pots or small gardens and contributes
to healthy soil and a happy insect population. You can also buy the petals
online or at health food stores.*

GF | NF | YR

If you feel a cold coming on or are suffering from a sore throat, this vividly coloured tea is a great way to get fluids in alongside some throat-soothing ingredients. This makes a large serving and I try to drink a full batch every day if I'm sick. It's spicy, fresh, and a little sweet—like an extravagant honey lemon tea. It helps that it looks like liquid sunshine, too, when you're feeling poorly.

Flu-Fighter Tea

Serves four | 5 minutes prep time | 15 minutes cooking time

4 cups (1 litre) water
2 thumbs ginger (each about 3 inches / 8 cm), sliced
1 thumb fresh turmeric (about 3 inches / 8 cm), sliced
2 cinnamon sticks
¼ teaspoon hot pepper flakes
Juice of 3 lemons
2 tablespoons honey
2 tablespoons bee pollen (optional)

Add the water, ginger, turmeric, cinnamon sticks, and hot pepper flakes to a large pot and bring to a boil. Reduce and simmer for 10 minutes. Strain, then whisk with lemon juice, honey, and bee pollen (if using). Serve hot.

NOTES
A thumb of ginger or turmeric is a piece approximately the size of your thumb, but some variation in size is fine.

If you can't find fresh turmeric, just leave it out. Powdered tastes strange in this recipe.

NF

I somehow became the cinnamon roll person when we moved to Germany. Though I'd been making them for well over a decade before then, no one else in my family in Germany does. My omi is obsessed with them but hates any addition to the classic recipe. No apple allowed and no nuts—only raisins, which I dislike. I think the mix of dates, apple, and tahini here, with all the extra spices, is fall in a nutshell, much more so than pumpkin pie. If you're a bread novice, cinnamon rolls are a good place to start despite the long rising time, since the dough is easy to work with.

Apple Cinnamon Spice Rolls

Makes about fourteen rolls | 20 minutes prep time |
90 minutes rising time | 30 minutes cooking time

Dough

1 cup (250 ml) non-dairy milk

3 tablespoons solid coconut oil

3 tablespoons maple syrup or honey

2¼ teaspoons dry yeast (½ cube fresh)

2½ to 3 cups (375 to 450 grams) light spelt flour, divided

1 teaspoon cinnamon

½ teaspoon salt

1 teaspoon grapeseed or avocado oil, to coat the bowl

Filling

2 tablespoons solid coconut oil, softened

2 tablespoons tahini

3 tablespoons maple syrup or honey

1 large apple, grated

¼ cup (60 grams) pitted chopped dates

1 tablespoon cinnamon

1 teaspoon freshly ground cardamom

½ teaspoon finely grated nutmeg

Heat the milk over medium-low heat in a small saucepan until warm to the touch. Remove from the heat and whisk in the coconut oil and maple syrup.

Pour the mixture into a large heatproof bowl and whisk in the yeast. Let it rest for 15 minutes, or until foaming. If, after 15 minutes, your yeast isn't foaming, you'll have to start again. Either the yeast was old (and dead) before starting, or the milk was too hot and it killed the yeast.

Stir in 1 cup (150 grams) of flour and the cinnamon and salt. Add the remaining flour in ½-cup (75-gram) increments, stirring between each addition, until it becomes too difficult to stir.

Turn the dough out onto a well-floured surface and knead, adding more flour as needed, until a soft and smooth dough forms. This should take about 10 minutes.

Pour the oil into a large bowl and place the dough in it, turning a few times to make sure the dough is coated. Cover with a plate and set the bowl in a warm place for the dough to rise for about 1 hour or until doubled in size.

recipe continues . . .

Line a baking sheet with parchment paper. Roll the dough out on a well-floured surface to about a ¾-inch (2 cm) thick square. Spread the coconut oil, tahini, and maple syrup over the dough, then top with the apple and dates and sprinkle with the cinnamon, cardamom, and nutmeg.

Lift the top one-third of the dough and fold it two-thirds of the way down, then fold up the bottom third to make a long rectangle. Think of how a pamphlet is folded. Cut the folded dough into 1-inch (2.5 cm) wide strips, cutting parallel to the short edge of the dough.

Twist the strips a few times, then roll into spirals from the centre outward, tucking the loose end underneath the roll (see note). They should look like snail shells.

Place the rolls on the prepared baking sheet and cover with a tea towel. Set them in a warm place to rise for 30 minutes, or until roughly doubled in size.

While the buns are rising, preheat your oven to 350°F (180°C). Once the buns have finished rising, place the baking sheet on the centre rack of the oven and bake for 25 to 30 minutes, or until golden.

Serve the rolls warm if you can, and keep leftovers in a sealed container at room temperature for up to 3 days.

NOTE
To simplify things, roll the filled dough into a log and cut into rounds instead of twisting.

GF | YR

*I did yoga teacher training
several years ago that included a
lot of meditation time. I quickly
discovered that I wasn't very good
at meditation—I do yoga more for
exercise—and during those quiet
periods, I thought of many, many
recipes. This ice cream cake was
one of them, and I'm so happy to
finally be sharing it, so many
years later. It is, despite the
healthy-ish ingredient list,
definitely an ice cream cake and
one of the most fun recipes
included in this book. With a
buttery pecan base layer, date
caramel, and a creamy, rich
chocolate ganache, it's over the
top and definitely worth it.*

Chocolate Caramel
Ice Cream Cake

Serves eight to ten | 15 minutes prep time | 10 minutes cooking time |
4 to 6 hours freezing time

Pecan Base

2 cups (300 grams) raw pecans
   (see note)

½ cup (120 grams) soft pitted
   dates

2 tablespoons coconut cream

2 tablespoons solid coconut oil

1 teaspoon vanilla extract

¼ teaspoon salt

Caramel

1 cup (240 grams) soft pitted
   dates

¼ cup (60 ml) coconut cream

½ teaspoon vanilla extract

1 tablespoon Nut and Seed
   Butter (page 240) or natural
   peanut butter

Chocolate Ganache

3½ ounces (100 grams) dark
   chocolate, chopped

1 can (13½ ounces / 400 ml)
   full-fat coconut milk

1 teaspoon vanilla extract

¼ teaspoon salt

Line an 8-inch (20 cm) springform pan with parchment paper and
set aside.

To make the pecan base, toast the pecans in a dry pan over medium
heat for about 5 minutes, stirring frequently. Cool for 10 minutes,
then add to a food processor and blend until a fine meal forms,
keeping the tube open to let any steam escape. Add the dates, coconut
cream, coconut oil, vanilla, and salt and pulse until the dates break
down and a dough comes together, a couple of minutes.

Press the pecan base into an even layer in the prepared pan and place
in the freezer while you prepare the other layers.

To make the caramel, place the dates, coconut cream, vanilla, and nut
and seed butter in a food processor and blend on high speed until very
smooth. Spread in an even layer over the pecan base and freeze until
hard, about 2 hours.

recipe continues . . .

For the ganache, place the chocolate in a large heatproof bowl and set aside.

Heat the coconut milk over medium-low heat in a small saucepan until simmering. Pour over the chocolate and let this sit for a full minute before whisking until glossy. Whisk in the vanilla and salt, and cool for 30 minutes at room temperature (see note).

Pour the ganache over the frozen caramel layer and freeze again until the top layer is set, 2 to 4 hours. When ready to serve, thaw for 10 minutes before slicing and serving, dipping your knife into hot water to help cut cleaner slices. This will keep for up to 2 weeks in a sealed container in the freezer.

NOTES

Walnuts can be substituted for pecans if preferred.

For the coconut cream, simply use the creamy top layer of a can of full-fat coconut milk.

If you want to make this even more like ice cream, churn the ganache mixture in an ice cream maker before layering onto the caramel and freezing fully.

NF | CE

This dessert is a bit sweeter than most of the recipes in this book, but a true pudding and a very enjoyable one. Clafoutis is surprisingly simple to make and a delight to eat—this is technically a flaugnarde, as it doesn't use cherries, but you could certainly make it in the summer with cherries, other berries, or apricots. Either way, this is a very relaxed dessert and can be made to your taste.

Blackberry Clafoutis

Serves six to eight | 10 minutes prep time | 45 minutes cooking time

3 large eggs

1 can (13½ ounces / 400 ml) full-fat coconut milk

1 teaspoon vanilla extract

½ cup (75 grams) light spelt flour

⅓ cup (55 grams) coconut sugar

Seeds of 1 cardamom pod, crushed (or ¼ teaspoon ground)

Pinch salt

2 cups (400 grams) blackberries

Preheat the oven to 400°F (200°C) and grease an 8-inch (20 cm) oven-safe baking dish or cast-iron pan.

Crack the eggs into a large bowl and whisk well until foaming. Add the coconut milk and vanilla and whisk again. Add the flour, sugar, cardamom, and salt, and gently mix.

Pour the batter into the prepared baking dish and scatter the berries over it in an even layer. Bake for 40 to 45 minutes, or until puffed up and golden. Cool for 10 minutes before serving warm or cold. This will keep well at room temperature, covered, for a couple of days.

Coconut Labneh Cake

Serves eight to ten | 10 minutes prep time | 1 hour cooking time

I was ecstatic to get this recipe right, or as right as a dairy-free cheesecake without processed "cheese" can be. Baked cheesecake like this, not like New York style, is a German staple, and labneh makes a surprisingly good substitute that's as close to quark as you can get. Topped with fresh figs, this cake is stunning in autumn. At other times of year, use berries, persimmons, stone fruits, or anything you like.

Cake Base

1 cup (110 grams) rolled oats

½ cup (75 grams) raw walnuts

¼ cup (60 grams) soft pitted dates

2 tablespoons solid coconut oil

2 tablespoons non-dairy milk

1 teaspoon vanilla extract

½ teaspoon cinnamon

¼ teaspoon salt

Labneh Filling

3 large eggs, yolks and whites separated

2 cups (350 grams) Coconut Labneh (from 2 batches of yogurt) (page 231)

½ cup (80 grams) coconut sugar

¼ cup (30 grams) oat flour

2 tablespoons arrowroot powder

2 teaspoons vanilla extract

Zest of 1 lemon

Juice of 1 lemon

2 tablespoons melted coconut oil

Halved figs and honey, for serving

Preheat the oven to 350°F (180°C) and grease an 8-inch (20 cm) springform pan with coconut oil.

To make the base, mix the oats and walnuts on high speed in a food processor until a flour forms. Add the dates, oil, milk, vanilla, cinnamon, and salt and blend again until well combined and slightly sticky. Press the base mixture in an even layer into the prepared pan, going about 2 inches (5 cm) up the sides. Set aside.

To make the filling, in a large bowl, whisk together the egg yolks, labneh, sugar, oat flour, arrowroot, vanilla, lemon zest, and lemon juice. Whisk in the coconut oil. In another bowl, beat the egg whites to stiff peaks. Use a spatula to fold the egg whites carefully into the labneh mixture, making sure not to knock the air out of the whites. It should be an even, fluffy mixture.

Pour the labneh filling over the cake base and gently shake to even it out. Bake for 55 to 60 minutes, until very golden. It might crack, and it will rise significantly before falling once removed from the oven. Don't open the oven while it's baking.

Cool fully before serving, topped with figs and a drizzle of honey. This keeps well, refrigerated in an airtight container, for up to 3 days.

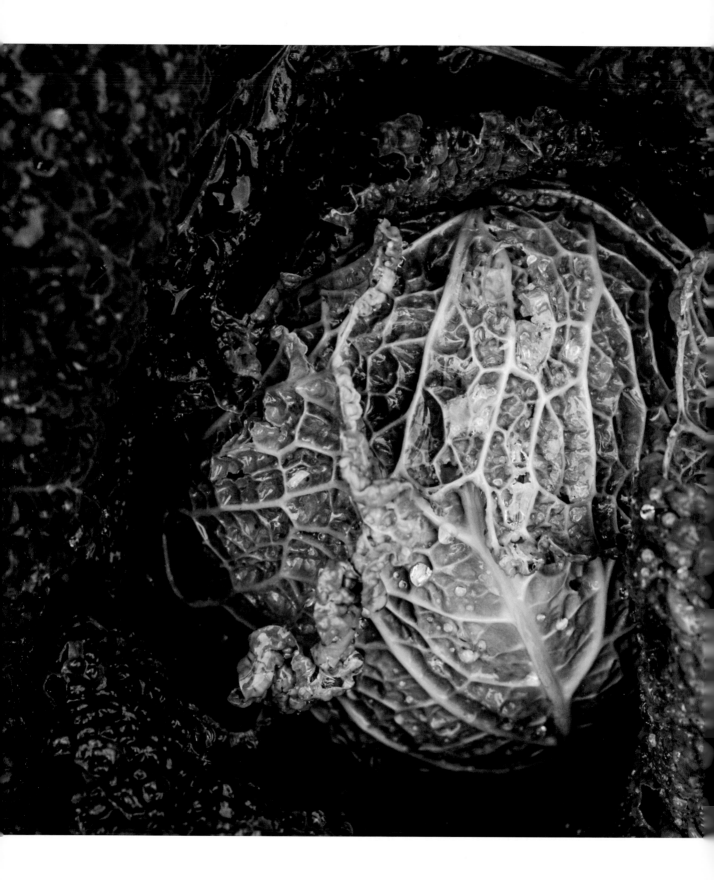

Winter

Winter is a difficult time of year for many. For me, it means a return of seasonal depression as an ongoing symptom of major depression, and I dread it every year. As soon as the days start to shorten—especially in northern Europe—it's a reminder that a long and dark season is ahead. I find winter in the prairies, although extraordinarily cold, to be much kinder. There, the sun is always out and the snow sparkles, but I have to say that I like to have kale in the garden in the middle of winter where I live in the Netherlands, even if it does rain every day.

Despite the less pleasant aspects of this dark and chilly season, there are still things to look forward to. Coziness in warm drinks, spices, and an abundance of soups. Warm bread and baking. I'm always more productive in the kitchen during winter because cooking is the only thing I'm really interested in doing. There's a word in Dutch, gezellig, and I think it suits winter if you let it. It means to be cozy, relaxed, and social, all in one. Use the time spent indoors to be cozy, let yourself hibernate a little, maybe work on some hobbies like baking. Invite a friend over for cake.

For food, colder weather means plenty of carbs, chocolate, and spice. While it can be a job and a half to get enough vegetables in the winter, there are some very fresh recipes in this chapter. I've incorporated seasonal fruits and vegetables, with the focus more on comfort food. Plenty of root vegetables are in season all winter, as are some hardy greens, and spices, dried fruits, and chocolate add flavour to otherwise simple ingredients. Oranges, persimmons, and pomegranate add some touches of brightness and sunshine. Warm drinks every day, either tea or hot chocolate, and maybe a cookie or two, make coming home from work or school in the dark more bearable.

I hope that this chapter encourages you to embrace this season through food, not by eating a whole batch of cookies because you're sad, but by enjoying the process of making the cookies. Then if you want to eat the whole batch, well, I don't judge. I do it, too.

GF | SF | YR

On-the-Run Breakfast Cookies

Makes ten cookies | 10 minutes prep time | 15 minutes cooking time

A little chewy, crumbly, and lightly sweet, this is a breakfast you'll be happy to have whether you're in a time crunch or having a slow morning. I make a variation of these almost every week to have on hand for snacks, using whatever's in the pantry. There are several options provided for these easily adaptable cookies, as they'll work with whatever you can throw at them. Although I've kept them gluten-free, spelt flour can be substituted for the other flour options.

1 cup (120 grams) oat, rice, or buckwheat flour

1 cup (110 grams) rolled oats or other flakes (see note)

½ cup (70 grams) seed or nut flour

½ cup (70 grams) mixed seeds or chopped nuts (see note)

¼ cup (50 grams) chia seeds

¼ cup (40 grams) dried fruit (such as raisins or dried berries)

1 teaspoon cinnamon

½ teaspoon salt

½ teaspoon baking soda

½ cup (120 grams) soft pitted dates

¼ cup (60 grams) solid coconut oil

¼ cup (50 grams) Nut and Seed Butter (page 240)

¼ cup (60 ml) non-dairy milk

Preheat the oven to 350°F (180°C). Grease a large baking sheet or line it with parchment paper.

Mix the oat flour, oats, seed flour, seeds, chia, dried fruit, cinnamon, salt, and baking soda in a large bowl.

Add the dates and oil to a food processor and mix until smooth. Add the nut and seed butter and milk and pulse to combine.

Use your hands or a spoon to stir the date mixture into the dry ingredients, making sure no streaks of flour remain.

Form the dough into ten equal balls and place on the prepared baking sheet. Press down gently to flatten to about 1¼ inches (3 cm) thick, then bake for 13 to 15 minutes, or until golden.

Cool for 10 minutes before removing from the sheet and cooling fully on a rack. These cookies will keep well for several days in a sealed container in a cool space, but should be refrigerated if your house is warm. They freeze well.

NOTE

Pumpkin, sunflower, and sesame seeds are all great, as are almonds, hazelnuts, and any other nuts you have on hand.

You could also use rye flakes, spelt flakes, or quinoa flakes instead of the rolled oats.

Slightly spicy chocolate and cinnamon, ginger, and a bit of cayenne take these from plain old chocolate muffins (also very good) to something a bit more interesting. These are sweetened with banana and dates, making them completely appropriate as a chocolate breakfast.

Mexican Chocolate Muffins

Makes twelve muffins | 10 minutes prep time | 25 minutes cooking time

1½ cups (225 grams) spelt flour

½ cup (50 grams) cocoa powder

2 teaspoons baking powder

½ teaspoon baking soda

2 teaspoons cinnamon

¼ teaspoon cayenne pepper

½ cup (120 grams) soft pitted dates

1 ripe banana

¼ cup (60 grams) solid coconut oil

1 teaspoon grated fresh ginger

1½ cups (375 ml) non-dairy milk

2 ounces (60 grams) dark chocolate, chopped, plus more for topping (optional for sugar-free)

Preheat the oven to 375°F (190°C). Grease a standard 12-cup muffin tin or line it with paper liners.

In a large bowl, whisk together the flour, cocoa, baking powder, baking soda, cinnamon, and cayenne.

Place the dates, banana, coconut oil, and ginger in the bowl of a food processor. Blend until a smooth paste forms, then add the milk and pulse until combined. Alternatively, mash well with a fork and stir in the milk.

Pour the date mixture over the dry ingredients and stir until just mixed. Gently fold in the chocolate (if using).

Divide the batter equally among the prepared muffin tin cups and top each with a sprinkle of chopped chocolate (if using).

Bake for 20 to 25 minutes, or until a toothpick inserted into the centre of a muffin comes out clean. Cool in the tin for about 5 minutes before removing and cooling fully on a rack. Keep refrigerated if your house is very warm. The muffins will keep well for up to 5 days in a cool place in a sealed container.

NF | SF | CE | YR

When Graham and I first moved to the Netherlands, we didn't have an oven, and for about a month, no stovetop either. My mom (angel that she is) surprised me with a toaster oven, and I made this recipe every couple of days, topped with roasted potatoes, carrots, and a tahini sauce. Not the most balanced of meals, perhaps, but a very comforting one. This is a perfect recipe to make in the shortest days of winter. If you prefer to keep things a little more veg-forward, use dark green vegetables instead of topping carbs with potatoes.

Oven Pancake

Serves two to four | 10 minutes prep time | 15 minutes cooking time

3 large eggs

½ cup (125 ml) non-dairy milk

½ cup (75 grams) light spelt flour

1 teaspoon herbes de Provence

½ teaspoon salt

½ teaspoon freshly ground pepper

1 tablespoon solid coconut oil

Basic Tahini Dressing (page 247)

Hardy greens or other vegetables (see note)

Place a cast-iron pan on the centre rack of your oven and preheat to 425°F (220°C). Both the pan and oven must be very hot before baking.

Add the eggs to a large bowl and whisk until foamy. Whisk in the milk, then add the flour, herbes de Provence, salt, and pepper, mixing until no lumps remain.

Carefully remove the hot pan from the oven and, working quickly, add the coconut oil. Once it's melted, pour the prepared batter into the pan.

Bake for 13 to 15 minutes, or until very puffy and golden. Serve with tahini dressing and greens or vegetables of choice.

NOTES

To make this sweet, replace the herbes de Provence with cinnamon and add 2 tablespoons of coconut sugar with the flour. Top with applesauce, pears, or jam.

I like to serve this very simply with arugula or spinach, since they don't need additional cooking before serving, but roasted vegetables (such as the Rosemary Roasted Roots on page 127) or wilted chard or kale are excellent as well. And roasted potatoes, too, of course.

NF | YR

If you've never tried coconut bread before, you're in for a treat. My childhood best friend was Trinidadian, and her family made coconut bread all the time. When my family moved to Manitoba, they gave me the recipe. The original was lost a few years ago in a fire, so this is my version. It's definitely a lighter version with the maple syrup, but it tastes just the way I remember.

Coconut Bread Muffins

Makes twelve muffins | 10 minutes prep time | 24 minutes cooking time

2 cups (300 grams) spelt flour

1½ cups (150 grams) unsweetened shredded coconut

2 teaspoons baking powder

½ teaspoon baking soda

1 teaspoon cinnamon

½ teaspoon freshly ground nutmeg

½ teaspoon ground cardamom

1 can (13½ ounces / 400 ml) full-fat coconut milk

¼ cup (60 ml) melted coconut oil

¼ cup (60 ml) maple syrup

1 teaspoon vanilla extract

Flaked coconut, for topping (optional)

Preheat the oven to 375°F (190°C). Grease a standard 12-cup muffin tin or line it with paper liners.

Add the flour, coconut, baking powder, baking soda, cinnamon, nutmeg, and cardamom to a large mixing bowl. Stir to combine.

Whisk together the coconut milk, coconut oil, maple syrup, and vanilla in a smaller bowl. Pour over the dry ingredients and stir until just mixed, with no streaks of flour remaining.

Divide the batter equally among the prepared muffin tin cups, topping with flaked coconut (if using). Bake for 22 to 24 minutes, or until golden or a toothpick inserted into the centre of a muffin comes out clean.

Cool for 10 minutes in the muffin tin before removing and cooling fully on a rack. Store in an airtight container for up to 5 days, or freeze for up to a month.

YR

Tahini Date Banana Bread

Makes one loaf | 10 minutes prep time | 50 minutes cooking time

The slight bitterness from the tahini against sweet bananas, maple syrup, and spices is pretty phenomenal here. I love banana bread but find that it can be a bit boring texturally, and this recipe ditches that altogether by using chewy dates, crunchy hazelnuts, and pockets of dark chocolate. It's a great everyday banana bread but special enough to make as a gift.

2 cups (300 grams) spelt flour

1 tablespoon baking powder

½ teaspoon baking soda

2 teaspoons cinnamon

½ teaspoon salt

¼ teaspoon freshly ground nutmeg

½ cup (75 grams) hazelnuts, coarsely chopped

¼ cup (60 grams) dates, pitted and coarsely chopped (see note)

2 ounces (60 grams) dark chocolate, chopped

2 medium overripe bananas

¼ cup (60 grams) tahini (see note)

¼ cup (60 ml) olive oil

¼ cup (60 ml) maple syrup

¾ cup (180 ml) non-dairy milk

Preheat the oven to 375°F (190°C) and grease a standard loaf tin (about 10 × 5 inches / 25 × 12 cm) with coconut oil.

In a large bowl, mix the flour, baking powder, baking soda, cinnamon, salt, and nutmeg. Stir in the hazelnuts, dates, and chocolate.

In a shallow bowl, mash the bananas with a fork. Stir in the tahini, oil, and maple syrup, followed by the milk.

Add the wet ingredients to the dry ingredients and stir until just mixed, with no streaks of flour remaining. Pour into the prepared tin and bake for 45 to 50 minutes, or until it passes the toothpick test (the toothpick should be mostly clean, but a little crumb is acceptable here) and the top is a dark golden colour.

Cool for 10 minutes in the tin before removing and cooling fully on a rack. The bread will cut into cleaner slices when fully cool, but tastes better warm, so use your discretion. The loaf will keep well for up to 3 days in a sealed container on the counter, and freezes well for up to a month.

NOTES

For this recipe I prefer harder dates that are easier to chop—time to reach for the ones forgotten at the back of the cupboard. Any dates will work, though.

Any nut or seed butter can be used in place of tahini for this recipe if you prefer. Tahini can sometimes feel a bit played out, but it has a subtler taste than peanut butter, which can often overwhelm everything else.

GF | NF | SF | YR

Crackers often seem like a lot of work for little reward. So much rolling into the very thinnest possible layer, cutting—it's all very fiddly. These seedy crackers need nothing more than a quick mix (in a single bowl) before baking. No cutting required for a crisp, flavour-packed snack. A very relaxed cracker indeed. Try them with hummus, cheese (or "cheese"), or soup, or however you'd normally eat crackers. This recipe is adapted from one of the first recipes I made from the Oh She Glows *blog, so long ago that it became a kitchen staple for me, and I forgot their origin!*

Seed Crackers

Makes a big batch, about twenty crackers | 5 minutes prep time | 1 hour cooking time

½ cup (100 grams) chia seeds

½ cup (70 grams) sunflower seeds

¼ cup (35 grams) sesame seeds

¼ cup (35 grams) flax seeds

1 cup (250 ml) water

2 tablespoons olive oil

1 tablespoon minced rosemary

1 teaspoon salt, plus more for topping

Preheat the oven to 320°F (160°C) and line a large baking sheet with parchment paper.

Mix the chia seeds, sunflower seeds, sesame seeds, flax seeds, water, oil, rosemary, and salt in a large bowl. It will be quite wet (see note). Spread the cracker mixture in an even layer on the baking sheet, about ¼ inch (5 mm) thick. Top with a sprinkle of salt.

Bake for 50 to 60 minutes, or until lightly golden. Make sure the middle is also golden, not only the edges. Cool completely on the sheet before breaking into pieces and storing. The crackers will keep well in a sealed container in a cool place for up to 2 weeks.

NOTES
These crackers will seem like an unidentifiable seed gel before baking, but I promise that they bake up crisp and crackable.

I never bother to cut the crackers, instead breaking them into pieces after baking, as they don't lend themselves very well to cutting into ordered squares.

NF | YR

Garlic Spelt Naan

Makes twelve pieces | 20 minutes prep time | 1 hour rising time |
10 minutes cooking time

Naan is one of the easiest bread recipes you can make at home. It needs only a single rise, it's easy to shape, and it's cooked in a frying pan instead of baked. I find that adding a little extra oil to the pan for each bread, plus a pinch of salt, really improves this recipe, but it certainly reduces the healthier aspect a touch. This version is soft and slightly chewy with a hint of a crisp on the outer layer, and the garlic takes things over the top. Serve this naan with any kind of curry or stew, like my Chickpea Parsnip Tajine (page 196) or Golden Pumpkin and Chickpea Stew (page 135), or with dishes like the Yoga Bowl (page 93).

NOTES
Garlic will prevent the dough from proofing fully if added earlier, so it's added after the first rise.

You can make these into buns for the Curry Burgers (page 199) simply by frying smaller and slightly thicker pieces of dough and cutting them in half.

¼ cup (60 ml) warm water

2¼ teaspoons dry yeast (½ cube fresh)

1 teaspoon coconut sugar

1 cup (250 ml) room-temperature water

2 tablespoons olive oil, plus more to coat the bowl

1 teaspoon salt

2½ to 3 cups (375 to 450 grams) spelt flour, divided

3 cloves garlic, minced

Coconut oil, for frying

In a large bowl, whisk together the ¼ cup (60 ml) warm water, yeast, and coconut sugar. Let the mixture sit for 15 minutes, until foaming. If, after 15 minutes, your yeast isn't foaming, you'll have to start again. Either the yeast was old (and dead) before starting, or the water was too hot and it killed the yeast.

Stir in the 1 cup (250 ml) room-temperature water, oil, salt, and 1 cup (150 grams) flour with a wooden spoon. Add the remaining flour ½ cup (75 grams) at a time, stirring between each addition, until it becomes too difficult to stir.

Turn the dough out onto a well-floured surface and flour your hands. Knead for 5 to 10 minutes, sprinkling additional flour as needed, until a soft and smooth dough forms. You can also use the dough hook in a stand mixer if you have one.

Grease a large bowl with olive oil and place the kneaded dough in it, brushing a little oil over the dough and covering with a tea towel. Place in a warm draft-free spot and let the dough rise for about 50 to 60 minutes, or until doubled in size.

Punch the dough down, then add the garlic and gently knead until it's incorporated evenly into the dough.

Heat a large frying pan on medium-high heat. Portion the dough into twelve equal pieces, then flour a clean work surface and roll out one piece of dough into a rough oval, about ¾ inch (2 cm) thick.

Once the pan is very hot, add about ½ teaspoon coconut oil, followed by the rolled dough. The dough should immediately bubble and start to puff up. Sprinkle a little pinch of salt over top, if desired, and cook for about 45 seconds. Lift the naan, add another ½ teaspoon oil to the pan, and flip.

While the first naan is cooking, roll out the second piece of dough to fry. Repeat until all of the dough has been rolled and fried, keeping the cooked flatbreads in a warm oven while cooking. The naan is best eaten fresh, but will still be good on day 2 if stored in a sealed container on the counter.

GF | NF | SF | YR

Caramelized Onion Hummus

Makes about 2 cups (425 grams) | 5 minutes prep time

A while back, I ended up with some leftover caramelized onions from another recipe. I tossed them into a batch of hummus to use them up, and loved it. They add a sweetness to the hummus—a nice change from the usual bite of fresh garlic. Because the recipe needs such a small amount of caramelized onions, this is the perfect thing to make when you have some leftovers.

2 cups (300 grams) soft chickpeas (see page 11), drained and rinsed

¼ cup (60 grams) tahini

Juice of 1 lemon

1 teaspoon salt

½ teaspoon ground cumin

½ teaspoon cayenne pepper

¼ cup (40 grams) Caramelized Onions (page 252), plus more for serving

1 tablespoon olive oil, plus more for serving

Sumac, for garnish (optional)

Freshly ground black pepper, for garnish (optional)

Add the chickpeas, tahini, lemon juice, salt, cumin, cayenne, and caramelized onions to a food processor and blend until smooth. Pour in the oil in a slow stream while blending, until the hummus is very light and fluffy.

Serve topped with a drizzle of olive oil, more caramelized onions, and a sprinkle of sumac and/or pepper (if using).

NOTE
This hummus makes a great simple pasta sauce! To make a creamy pasta, add a generous amount of the hummus to noodles of your choice with ¼ cup (60 ml) of the pasta cooking water and some peas or greens for a quick, wholesome dinner.

GF | NF | SF

This recipe is a great way to have fresh salsa even in the dead of winter. Persimmons are a welcome alternative to tomatoes—they have some of the same properties, and they offer a hint of sunshine in their colour, a reminder that winter doesn't last forever. Eat this the way you would regular salsa, with tortilla chips, on tacos, or as a side to some naan.

Persimmon Salsa

Serves five to six | 10 minutes prep time

1½ cups (200 grams) chopped persimmons

1 small red onion, minced

1 clove garlic, minced

Juice of 1 lime

1 tablespoon olive oil

½ teaspoon salt

½ teaspoon freshly ground pepper

Add the persimmons, onions, garlic, lime juice, oil, salt, and pepper to a bowl and mix. This can be eaten immediately, but I like to let it sit for 30 to 60 minutes to mellow the onions before serving. It can be kept for a day, refrigerated, in a sealed container.

NOTE

There are a couple of common types of persimmons. Fuyu are squat and can be consumed when still firm, whereas Hachiya are elongated and must ripen until very soft before eating. Look for fruits without bruises, especially with Hachiya, as you'll likely have them for some time before eating them. They can be stored at room temperature until ripe. I've used both when making this recipe, so go with your preference or what you can find.

GF | NF | SF | YR

Cacao Date Spread

Makes about 1½ cups (300 grams) | 5 minutes prep time |
20 minutes cooking time

This recipe came about from a chocolate craving and a general laziness that prevented me from going out and buying a chocolate bar. It tastes like chocolate fruit—as if a date palm and a chocolate bar were grafted into one tree—and should ideally be eaten with liberal amounts of toast. This is quite sweet (from the natural sugar in the dates, to be fair), but there is balance from the bitter cacao.

1 cup (250 ml) non-dairy milk (oat, or coconut for extra richness)

1 cup (240 grams) pitted dates

1 tablespoon coconut oil

¼ cup (25 grams) raw cacao powder

Tiny pinch salt

Place the milk and dates in a small saucepan. Bring to a low boil over medium heat, then reduce and simmer, covered, for about 20 minutes, until the dates are very soft. If the milk is evaporating quickly and the dates aren't yet soft, add another splash of milk.

Remove from the heat. Add the coconut oil, cacao powder, and salt to the saucepan and use an immersion blender (or transfer to a small heat-safe blender; see note) to blend until smooth. Store in a sealed container in the refrigerator for up to a week.

NOTES

To turn this into a healthier chocolate hazelnut spread, mix in ½ cup (100 grams) hazelnut butter when blending.

One of my recipe testers noted that this was near impossible to make in her high-powered blender, so a small one is needed, or a doubling of the recipe.

Bean and Barley Soup

Serves six | 10 minutes prep time | 1 hour cooking time

My aunt lived just up the (gravel) road from us and still lives a couple of farms away from my parents, and I spent a lot of time at her house as a child. Aunt Joyce influenced my love of gardening and foraging, taking me to pick saskatoon berries, teaching me how to help in her large kitchen garden, and inspiring a love for preserving. She'd hate that I use beans in this soup instead of the traditional beef—she's a retired cattle farmer, after all—but she'd forgive me, I think. It might seem mundane, but there's truly nothing better in the middle of winter than this warm hug of a soup, with layers of flavour from the herbs and dried mushrooms, creamy beans, and slightly toothsome barley.

2 teaspoons olive oil

1 large onion, diced

3 medium carrots, cut into ½-inch (1 cm) slices

1 turnip, peeled and diced

2 cloves garlic, minced

1 tablespoon apple cider vinegar

5 cups (1.25 litres) Vegetable Stock (page 243)

¼ cup (20 grams) dried mushrooms, chopped (optional)

½ cup (80 grams) barley (see note)

3 tablespoons thyme leaves, plus more for serving

2 bay leaves

1 teaspoon salt

1 teaspoon freshly ground pepper

1 teaspoon herbes de Provence

2 cups (300 grams) cooked or canned white beans, drained and rinsed

Spring Onion Biscuits (page 35), for serving

Heat a large pot over medium heat. Add the oil, followed by the onions, and cook for about 5 minutes, stirring frequently, until translucent. Stir in the carrots and turnips and cook for another 5 minutes. Add the garlic and stir to brown slightly, cooking for another 30 seconds.

Pour in the vinegar, followed by the stock. Bring to a rolling boil. Add the mushrooms (if using), barley, thyme, bay leaves, salt, pepper, and herbes de Provence. Reduce to a simmer and cook for 45 to 50 minutes, or until the barley is cooked.

Stir in the beans to heat through. Serve hot, topped with extra thyme and with biscuits on the side. The soup will keep well for a day or two at room temperature or refrigerated, and freezes well for up to a month.

NOTE

Barley benefits from a soak ahead of time if you can manage it. Try to soak it anywhere between 4 and 24 hours for a shorter cooking time, about 30 minutes instead of 45 minutes. This will also help prevent the grain from soaking up any broth when storing leftovers, which it has a tendency to do.

NF | SF

Cold-Weather Noodle Soup

Serves four to six | 10 minutes prep time | 30 minutes cooking time

Noodle soup is a winter staple. This is my version of my mom's chicken noodle soup, and it's virtually the same, just with beans in place of chicken. It's comforting whether you have a cold or not, and exactly what's needed on cold winter days. With warming ginger, vibrant lemon, and a handful of herbs, it's a cozy soup with a fresh twist.

1 teaspoon olive oil

1 small onion, diced

2 carrots, sliced into ½-inch (1 cm) rounds

3 stalks celery, cut into ½-inch (1 cm) pieces

3 cloves garlic, minced

1 tablespoon minced fresh ginger

1 teaspoon salt

½ teaspoon hot pepper flakes

½ teaspoon freshly ground pepper

6 cups (1.5 litres) Vegetable Stock (page 243)

1½ cups (225 grams) cooked or canned chickpeas or white beans, drained and rinsed

1½ cups (100 grams) short pasta (such as fusilli, macaroni, or cavatappi)

Zest of 1 lemon

Juice of 1 lemon

3 cups (70 grams) chopped hardy greens (such as kale, chard, or spinach)

½ cup (30 grams) chopped parsley or cilantro

Basic Spelt Sourdough (page 223), for serving (optional)

Heat the oil in a large pot over medium heat. Add the onions and cook for 2 minutes, until they begin to soften. Add the carrots and celery and cook for another 5 minutes. Stir in the garlic, ginger, salt, pepper flakes, and pepper and cook for an additional minute.

Pour in the stock and bring to a rolling boil. Add the chickpeas, reduce to a simmer, and cook, covered, for 10 minutes.

Increase the heat to bring to a boil again, and add the pasta. Reduce and cook on a low boil, stirring occasionally, until the pasta is cooked, about another 10 minutes or according to package instructions. Remove from the heat and stir in the lemon zest, lemon juice, greens, and parsley. Taste and season if necessary, and serve hot with sourdough, if desired.

This keeps well, refrigerated, for up to 3 days, if the pasta is cooked separately and added when reheating. The soup can also be frozen for a month without the pasta.

NOTE
You can easily make this gluten-free by using a gluten-free pasta. I like red lentil or brown rice pasta.

NF | SF

Northern Caesar Salad

Serves four | 10 minutes prep time | 20 minutes cooking time

Rye croutons, a kale base, and a sunflower seed parmesan "cheese" make this a very northern-climate-friendly salad, and it's a welcome addition to the winter table. Seaweed brings a slightly piscine flavour, while capers add extra salt to imitate anchovies in this vegan Caesar dressing, which I make creamy with hemp hearts.

4 cups (80 grams) stemmed and chopped kale

Creamy Hemp Dressing

¼ cup (40 grams) hemp hearts

1 clove garlic

2 teaspoons capers

1 teaspoon seaweed flakes (optional)

Zest of 1 lemon

Juice of 1 lemon

2 tablespoons water

1 tablespoon white wine vinegar

1 teaspoon Dijon mustard

½ teaspoon freshly ground pepper

¼ teaspoon salt

2 tablespoons olive oil

Rye Croutons

2 thick slices Scandinavian Dark Rye (page 227), cut into 1-inch (2.5 cm) cubes

1 tablespoon olive oil

2 cloves garlic, minced

¼ teaspoon salt

Sunflower Seed Parmesan

¼ cup (35 grams) sunflower seeds

3 tablespoons hemp hearts

1 clove garlic

1 teaspoon olive oil

¼ teaspoon salt

Place the kale in a large bowl and set aside. Preheat the oven to 375°F (190°C).

To make the dressing, place the hemp hearts, garlic, capers, seaweed flakes (if using), lemon zest, lemon juice, water, vinegar, mustard, pepper, and salt in a small food processor or in a tall container if you're using an immersion blender. Blend until smooth, then pour in the oil in a slow stream while blending. Taste and season if necessary.

To make the croutons, place the bread cubes on a large baking sheet and sprinkle with the oil, garlic, and salt. Use your hands to mix until the bread is well coated. Bake for 15 to 20 minutes, or until crisp. Set aside.

To make the parmesan, place the sunflower seeds, hemp hearts, garlic, oil, and salt in a small food processor. Blend until a coarse meal forms.

To assemble the salad, mix the dressing with the kale. Use your hands to massage for about 30 seconds to soften the kale slightly. Top with the croutons and parmesan, and serve. Leftovers hold up surprisingly well for up to 1 day, refrigerated in a sealed container.

Harissa No-Meat Balls

Makes about sixteen balls | 10 minutes prep time |
At least 1 hour soaking time | 20 minutes cooking time

I make a version of these easy lentil balls at least once a week, year-round. Harissa adds complexity to these without your having to reach for a number of spices, and increases the moisture content. The process can be sped up even more if you have a jar of harissa in the refrigerator. These are the vegan equivalent to chicken and go with absolutely everything—salad, pasta, fries, or veg (anything from carrot sticks to roasted broccoli)— and they need so little time, just right for a last-minute dinner. This is why you should freeze pre-soaked red lentils! These are a real crowd-pleaser—everyone, from my friend's five-year-old to my seventy-five-year-old oma, loves them.

1 cup (200 grams) dried red lentils, soaked (see note)

1 small red onion, quartered

2 cloves garlic

½ cup (30 grams) parsley

½ cup (60 grams) chickpea flour

2 tablespoons olive oil

2 tablespoons Harissa (page 244)

Juice of 1 lemon

1 teaspoon salt

½ teaspoon freshly ground pepper

Preheat the oven to 400°F (200°C) and line a baking sheet with parchment paper. Drain and rinse the lentils well in a fine-mesh sieve.

Place the onions, garlic, and parsley in a food processor and blend until finely chopped. Add the drained and rinsed lentils, flour, oil, harissa, lemon juice, salt, and pepper and blend until the mixture is almost smooth, with some lentil pieces remaining.

Form the mixture into golf-ball-sized balls and place on the baking sheet. They don't spread much, so don't worry about crowding. Bake for 18 to 20 minutes, until golden brown and quite firm.

NOTES

To do a quick soak, cover the lentils in very hot water for about 1 hour. Otherwise, soak overnight in cool water.

Don't have chickpea flour? Use rye instead with the same results—though the balls will no longer be gluten-free.

If you want to fry these instead of baking, add an egg to the mixture before blending and spoon directly into a hot pan with a drizzle of oil. Cook for a couple of minutes on each side, until golden.

To make these into burgers, form four patties about ¾ inch (2 cm) thick and bake for 25 to 30 minutes, until golden brown and quite firm.

NF | SF

Winter Vegetable Pot Pie

Serves four to six | 20 minutes prep time | 45 minutes cooking time

Creamy, with meaty mushrooms and hearty winter vegetables, this dish is a dream on the coldest nights of the year. Root vegetables are best, and sweetest, during winter. Added to a pie like this, they're given licence to shine. Pot pies always seem like a lot of work—anything involving pastry does—but the active time needed for this recipe is short, and well worth it.

Pot Pie Filling

1 tablespoon olive oil

3 cups (300 grams) thinly sliced button mushrooms

1 medium yellow onion, diced

2 medium carrots, cut into ½-inch (1 cm) slices

2 medium parsnips, cut into ½-inch (1 cm) slices

1 turnip or small celeriac, cut into ¾-inch (2 cm) pieces

2 cloves garlic, minced

3 tablespoons chickpea flour

1½ cups (375 ml) Vegetable Stock (page 243)

1½ cups (375 ml) Oat Cream (page 237)

¼ cup (15 grams) thyme leaves

Pastry

2 cups (300 grams) light spelt flour

½ teaspoon salt

¼ cup (60 grams) solid coconut oil

6 to 8 tablespoons cold water

Heat a medium-large oven-safe skillet or a pot over medium heat. Add the oil, followed by the mushrooms. Sear the mushrooms for about 5 minutes, or until golden brown, stirring once halfway through. The mushrooms should release a significant amount of water. Add the onions, carrots, parsnips, turnips, and garlic. Cook, stirring frequently, for 10 minutes. The vegetables will not be tender after this point but will cook fully in the oven.

Stir in the chickpea flour and cook for 30 seconds. Add the stock, oat cream, and thyme and simmer for another 5 minutes, until thickened. If you need to, transfer the filling into an oven-safe dish. Set aside while you make the pastry.

Preheat the oven to 400°F (200°C).

To make the pastry, mix the flour and salt in a large bowl. Use your hands or a pastry cutter to rub or cut in the oil to form pea-sized crumbs, then stir in the water a tablespoon at a time until a loose dough forms. It should hold when pressed between your fingers.

Roll the pastry out on a lightly floured surface to ½ inch (1 cm) thick. Cut the pastry to fit the pan, and place over the filling, then use a sharp knife to add a couple of cuts to the pastry to act as vents. Bake for 30 minutes, or until golden and bubbling. Cool for 10 minutes before serving.

NOTES

If you eat eggs, adding an egg wash will make the pastry more golden.

To make the most of your dough scraps, sprinkle them with coconut sugar and cinnamon and bake them for about 15 minutes at 375°F (190°C) (another lesson from my aunt Joyce, the pie queen).

NF | SF

Chickpea Parsnip Tajine

Serves four | 10 minutes prep time | 40 minutes cooking time

A tajine is a slow-cooked stew made in a specific earthenware dish (called a tajine, surprise surprise), often including dried fruit and heaps of spices. Fruit adds sweetness to what might otherwise be a single-tone dish. Traditional versions usually include lamb or chicken, but this is one of those dishes that's easy to turn into an extraordinary vegetarian meal. Chickpeas are a good vehicle for the spices, but this is still a surprisingly mellow dish despite the long ingredients list.

1 teaspoon olive oil

1 small onion, halved and thinly sliced

3 medium parsnips, halved and cut into ¾-inch (2 cm) slices

2 medium carrots, cut into ¾-inch (2 cm) rounds

3 cloves garlic, minced

1 teaspoon salt

1 teaspoon cinnamon

½ teaspoon ground turmeric

½ teaspoon cumin seeds

½ teaspoon sweet paprika

½ teaspoon cayenne pepper

2 cups (300 grams) cooked or canned chickpeas, drained and rinsed

2 cups (500 ml) Vegetable Stock (page 243)

¼ teaspoon saffron threads (optional)

¼ cup (50 grams) prunes

¼ cup (50 grams) dried apricots

To Serve

Chopped cilantro

Garlic Spelt Naan (page 178)

Coconut Yogurt (page 228)

Heat the oil in a large pot (or tajine) over medium heat. Add the onions and sauté for 2 to 3 minutes, or until softened and slightly golden. Stir in the parsnips and carrots and cook for another 5 minutes to soften slightly. Add the garlic, salt, cinnamon, turmeric, cumin, paprika, and cayenne, and stir.

Add the chickpeas, followed by the stock, saffron (if using), prunes, and dried apricots. Bring to a low boil and simmer, covered, for 25 to 30 minutes, or until the vegetables are tender.

Taste and season as needed. Serve hot with cilantro, naan, and yogurt. Leftovers keep well for a couple of days in the refrigerator.

SF | YR

Veggie burgers and pizza are Graham's favourite foods, and although I most often make the Harissa No-Meat Balls (page 192) into burgers, a proper burger with all the toppings is really something. With any plant based burger, strong flavour is key, and a good blend of curry, cashews, and plenty of complementary toppings make these burgers anything but boring. Because no one wants a burger that falls apart, the rice and chickpea flour keep it all together and the burgers are baked for extra insurance.

Curry Burgers

Makes six burgers | 10 minutes prep time | 25 minutes cooking time

1 small yellow onion, quartered

3 cloves garlic

2 cups (50 grams) hardy greens, torn into small pieces

½ cup (30 grams) cilantro

1½ cups (225 grams) cooked or canned chickpeas, drained and rinsed

1 cup (200 grams) cooked brown rice (see page 11)

¼ cup (40 grams) cashews

2 tablespoons chickpea flour

2 tablespoons olive oil

Juice of 1 lime

2 teaspoons Curry Spice Blend (page 248)

1 teaspoon salt

To Serve

Garlic Spelt Naan buns (see note on page 178)

Thinly sliced red onion or Pickled Red Onions (page 254)

Cilantro, chopped if desired

Spicy Orange Sauerkraut (page 232)

Coconut Labneh (page 231)

Preheat the oven to 350°F (180°C) and grease a baking sheet or line it with parchment paper.

Place the onions, garlic, greens, and cilantro in a food processor and blend until finely chopped. Add the chickpeas, rice, cashews, flour, oil, lime juice, curry blend, and salt and pulse until a textured dough forms, not blending too finely.

Divide the dough into six equal balls and form into patties 1 inch (2.5 cm) thick. Place on the prepared baking sheet and bake for 22 to 25 minutes, or until golden. Serve on naan buns with pickled onions, cilantro, sauerkraut, labneh, or any other favourite toppings, if desired.

NOTE
Arugula, spinach, kale, and chard can all be used as greens here.

GF | NF | SF

I grow kale and chard to overwinter, seeing as these types of greens are at their best during the cold months. I often make this smoothie to keep up my greens consumption when really I just want potatoes, and this is a great way to bring in more greens when you might feel like the weather is preventing you. It's refreshing without being cold, because the idea of a cold smoothie in the depths of winter is laughable. Ginger brightens things up, pear replaces banana, and hemp adds oomph. It's not a creamy drink, but is just cozy enough for winter mornings.

Winter Green

Serves one or two | 5 minutes prep time

2 cups (40 grams) baby greens

1 ripe pear, cored

1 cup (250 ml) coconut water

1 teaspoon grated fresh ginger

3 tablespoons hemp hearts

1 soft date, pitted (optional)

Add the greens, pear, coconut water, ginger, hemp hearts, and date (if using) to a blender and blend until smooth. Serve at room temperature.

NOTE
Any kind of hardy green can be used. Kale, chard, spinach, and arugula are all good.

GF | NF | SF

Winter Spice Tea

Makes about 1 cup (60 grams) loose tea | 10 minutes prep time | 1½ hours cooking time

A good spice tea is a winter staple. With jewel-like dried orange pieces, raisins, and aromatic spices, it brings a sense of warmth and colour to cold, dark days. This one is mildly spicy, with a strong orange flavour and chai undertones. It makes a beautiful gift to yourself or someone else, and is a very good replacement for store-bought fruit or spice teas, which often include mysterious additional flavouring and added sugar.

2 oranges, quartered and thinly sliced

¼ cup (40 grams) raisins

2 cinnamon sticks, broken into pieces

2 tablespoons star anise pieces

1 tablespoon cloves

1 tablespoon cracked cardamom pods

Preheat the oven to 250°F (120°C) and line a large baking sheet with parchment paper. Place the orange slices on the sheet and bake for 1 to 1½ hours, or until no longer sticky to touch.

In a large bowl, mix the dried oranges with the raisins, cinnamon sticks, star anise, cloves, and cardamom pods and store in a paper bag for up to 3 months.

To steep, use 2 tablespoons tea for 1 cup boiling water, or ¼ cup tea for a pot.

NOTE

If you prefer, you can cut strips or stamp small shapes from the peels of a couple of oranges instead of drying full slices. This has two benefits. One, the small pieces can be dried without an oven simply by placing them in a sunny place. Two, you get to eat the oranges!

GF | NF | YR

Dark Hot Chocolate

Serves two | 2 minutes prep time | 5 minutes cooking time

This is a basic recipe for vegan hot chocolate, but one that can easily be jazzed up with seasonal flavours. On its own, it's rich, slightly foamy, and a welcome treat when it's cold outside. Add other elements to suit your taste. I recommend cinnamon, nutmeg, cardamom, and orange zest—go ahead and get festive. Try topping it off with Whipped Coconut Cream (page 256) for extra decadence.

2 cups (500 ml) non-dairy milk (see note)

2 tablespoons cacao butter (see note)

3 tablespoons raw cacao powder

1 tablespoon maple syrup

½ teaspoon vanilla extract

Tiny pinch salt

Place the milk in a small saucepan over medium-high heat and bring to a low boil. Remove from the heat and stir in the cacao butter until melted.

Add the cacao powder, maple syrup, vanilla, and salt and whisk or blend with an immersion blender until very foamy and emulsified, a couple of minutes whisking or 30 seconds with a blender. Serve immediately.

NOTES
Cashew Milk (page 238) or coconut milk are best for this recipe thanks to their creamy nature, but any other milk will be fine. Homemade oat milk tends to thicken when heated.

Don't have cacao butter? Use three squares of dark chocolate (1 ounce / 30 grams) instead of the cacao butter and powder for the same results, minus some of the benefits of raw cacao.

Occasionally Eggs

GF | YR

Tahini Chocolate Chunk Cookies

Makes about twelve cookies | 10 minutes prep time |
12 minutes cooking time

This one took a lot of testing, but I'm not complaining. Even mediocre cookies are better than no cookies. These are excellent while being both vegan and gluten-free. Chewy, with slightly crisp edges, they rise and fall during baking as good chocolate chunk cookies should. Tahini doesn't add an overwhelming flavour to these and pairs well with the caramel notes of coconut sugar and the dark chocolate. I didn't set out to make these without gluten, but I tried a mix of oat and almond flour when I ran out of spelt and found they're better this way.

½ cup (60 grams) oat flour

½ cup (50 grams) almond flour

½ cup (80 grams) coconut sugar

1 tablespoon arrowroot powder

½ teaspoon salt

¼ teaspoon baking soda

½ cup (120 grams) runny tahini

2 tablespoons olive oil

2 tablespoons non-dairy milk

1 teaspoon vanilla extract

3½ ounces (100 grams) dark chocolate, chopped

Preheat the oven to 375°F (190°C) and line a large baking sheet with parchment paper.

Stir together the oat flour, almond flour, sugar, arrowroot powder, salt, and baking soda in a large bowl. In a smaller bowl, whisk together the tahini, oil, milk, and vanilla.

Add the wet ingredients to the dry ingredients and stir with a wooden spoon until mixed. Fold in the chocolate.

Scoop about 2 tablespoons of dough for each cookie and place on the prepared baking sheet, 2 inches (5 cm) apart. Bake for 10 to 12 minutes, or until golden. Cool for 5 minutes on the sheet before removing and cooling fully on a rack. They will be slightly delicate until cooled fully. Store in a sealed container at room temperature for up to a week, or freeze for up to a month.

NOTES

If you prefer, you can substitute natural peanut butter for the tahini. I often do!

If your tahini is quite thick and solid, you will need to add more milk to make up for the loss of moisture. The dough should be soft, not crumbly, and form one large ball when mixed. If it is crumbly due to dry tahini, add a tablespoon of milk at a time as needed.

NF | CE | YR

A Real Holiday Stunner

Makes one cake | 15 minutes prep time | 55 minutes cooking time

This replaced another recipe, I think a cookie, and when I emailed my editor about the switch, I jokingly called it "a real holiday stunner." She said I could include it as long as I kept the title, so here we are. It's a German-inspired spice cake with a hint of orange and snowy glaze. Upside-down rosemary is a typical winter decoration for good reason; it's easy, pretty, and doesn't affect the flavour of the cake.

Cake

2¼ cups (340 grams) light spelt flour

2 teaspoons baking powder

½ teaspoon baking soda

2 teaspoons cinnamon

½ teaspoon freshly ground nutmeg

½ teaspoon freshly ground cardamom

½ teaspoon ground ginger

½ teaspoon ground coriander

½ teaspoon salt

2 eggs

½ cup (125 ml) non-dairy milk

½ cup (125 ml) orange juice

½ cup (125 ml) olive oil

½ cup (125 ml) maple syrup

1 teaspoon vanilla extract

Glaze

¾ cup (180 ml) thick Coconut Yogurt (page 228) or Coconut Labneh (page 231)

Zest of 1 orange

Juice of 1 orange (about 3 tablespoons)

1 tablespoon maple syrup

5 to 6 rosemary sprigs, for topping

Preheat the oven to 350°F (180°C) and grease an 8-inch (20 cm) springform pan with coconut oil.

In a large bowl, sift together the flour, baking powder, baking soda, cinnamon, nutmeg, cardamom, ginger, coriander, and salt. Set aside.

In another bowl, beat the eggs until foaming. Whisk in the milk, orange juice, oil, maple syrup, and vanilla until well combined.

Add the wet ingredients to the dry ingredients and mix until just combined. Pour into the prepared pan and bake for 50 to 55 minutes, or until golden brown and a toothpick inserted into the middle of the cake comes out clean. Cool for 10 minutes in the pan before removing the sides of the pan and cooling fully on a rack.

Once the cake is cool, place parchment paper under the rack and prepare the glaze. Whisk the yogurt, orange zest and juice, and maple syrup together and pour over the cake. The glaze will drizzle down the sides if you encourage it to.

Place the glazed cake on a stand or platter. Top with upside-down rosemary sprigs to resemble pine trees, and serve immediately. Store the unglazed cake in a sealed container at room temperature for up to 3 days. Store the glazed cake in a container in the refrigerator.

NOTE

To make this cake to serve later or the following day, don't glaze it ahead of time (the glaze can be made ahead, but store it separately, refrigerated in a sealed container). The glaze has a tendency to sink into the cake and should be added immediately before serving.

GF | NF | YR

Raw Chocolate, How You Like It

Makes one large bar | 5 minutes prep time | 5 minutes cooking time

Raw chocolate is a little softer than what you might expect, but freezing it creates a snappy texture. Topped with whatever you like, it can be anything from a plain bar to outrageously decadent. This is my base recipe for homemade raw chocolate, which is shockingly expensive to buy in stores. Raw cacao is supposed to have a host of health benefits, and I like to use that as an excuse to eat masses of this chocolate once a month. Have it plain or be generous with the toppings; it's good either way.

¼ cup (50 grams) cacao butter

2 tablespoons raw honey

⅓ cup (35 grams) raw cacao powder

½ teaspoon vanilla extract

Tiny pinch salt

Possible Toppings

Dried fruits or freeze-dried fruits (strawberries, raspberries, mangoes)

Granola

Cinnamon

Pomegranate seeds

Orange zest

Chopped hazelnuts, cashews, or almonds

Shredded coconut

Place a square of parchment paper on a cutting board or line a small square or rectangular dish with parchment paper. Alternatively, you can use an ice cube tray or silicone moulds for individual chocolates.

Fill a small saucepan with 1 inch (2.5 cm) of water. Place a heatproof bowl over the pot and add the cacao butter to the bowl. Slowly melt the butter over medium-low heat.

Whisk in the honey, cacao powder, vanilla, and salt until well combined. Pour into a thin layer on the parchment paper (or into the moulds) and top with your desired toppings. Freeze until hardened, then break into small pieces before storing in the freezer in a sealed container. This will keep in the freezer for up to 2 weeks.

NOTE
To make milk chocolate, add 2 tablespoons nut butter when adding the cacao powder. It will be slightly softer, almost fudge-like. I recommend hazelnut butter.

Fermented

I didn't grow up with fermented foods, unless you count the awful sauerkraut that comes in a plastic bag. Sauerkraut was one of my most hated foods—it didn't help that my mom always served it with pork—but now I love it. Like most dishes, fermented foods are often better when you make them yourself. I started experimenting with sourdough several years ago, and fell in love. Later I started with ginger beer, and then kombucha, followed by yogurts and fermented vegetables. Like you might, I screwed up more times than I can count. Persistence is key, and now there's always something bubbling away on the counter.

There are many good reasons to ferment food. Most importantly, it's so much fun. It really feels like a science experiment or kitchen magic. To see a sourdough starter go from simple flour and water to beautiful loaf of crusty bread feels like a miracle every time. Bubbles forming from what seems to be nothing, creating natural soda pop; coconut milk turning into yogurt—incredible.

Other reasons are well documented, including the health benefits. Fermented food is all around better for our bodies—though without a nutrition degree, I don't want to get too much into that. I know that I feel much better after scarfing half a loaf of sourdough versus a yeasted bread (which also has a very important place in my kitchen). It's a good way to preserve foods, especially when refrigeration space is at a premium, and it tastes great.

Fermentation, and preserving as a whole, is one of the best ways to store the bounty of a specific season or garden abundance. Though we sometimes think of fermented foods as belonging more to winter, as they would traditionally be used as a source of vitamins during the months when a garden lies dormant, they're enjoyable and delicious year-round. You'll find fermented foods in recipes throughout this book, in every season.

Fermenting, in general, needs only the simplest of ingredients, and no special equipment is needed for these recipes. If you're just starting out, ginger beer is the way to go. It uses minimal and easy-to-find ingredients, it's simple to make, and it doesn't require any special skills. Both sourdough recipes are easy, too. And if you'd like to make fermented bread but aren't quite ready for a starter yet, both recipes in this book include instructions using yeast.

The sourdough recipes were created with beginners in mind. They do call for whole grain, lower-gluten flours, which can be harder to work with, but create a wonderfully rich and hearty loaf. (I'm a bit fast and loose with sourdough, which may shock every-gram-accounted-for bakers.)

So go, get fermenting, and have fun with it.

ginger beer

Ginger Bug and Ginger Beer

Makes 2 pints (1 litre) | 10 minutes prep time | 15 minutes cooking time |
5 days (ginger bug) plus 3 to 10 days (ginger beer) fermenting time

A ginger bug is like a sourdough starter. It's fed daily, and using a little kick-starts the fermentation process for the beer. Homemade ginger beer is spicy and not too sweet, especially this version, sweetened largely with apple juice. I've tried with honey but it doesn't produce consistent results. If you like carbonated drinks, this is like a healthier soda pop and great to add to a number of drinks and cocktails, like the floats on page 56. Ginger beer is probably the easiest thing to ferment at home.

Ginger Bug, for Each Feeding

1 teaspoon finely grated fresh
  ginger
1 teaspoon cane sugar
3 teaspoons water

Ginger Beer

3 cups (750 ml) water
1 large piece ginger (about
  6 inches / 15 cm), sliced
¼ cup (60 ml) ginger bug
Juice of 1 lemon
1 cup (250 ml) apple juice

To make the ginger bug, add the ginger, sugar, and water to a jam jar or container—the 8-ounce (250 ml) Ball jars are ideal—and stir to dissolve the sugar. Cover with a thin cloth and secure to keep any insects out.

Feed your bug the same amounts of ginger, sugar, and water on a daily basis, and you should see strong bubbling action after about 5 days. Once it's very bubbly, it's ready to use for the ginger beer. Continue to feed daily if you want to make a batch of ginger beer about once a week. If you plan on making ginger beer less frequently, refrigerate the bug until you want to use it, then feed once and leave it on the counter to use the next day (see note).

Sterilize a 2-pint (1 litre) bottle with a flip-top. You can use boiling water or run it through a dishwasher cycle.

To make the ginger beer, add the water and ginger to a large pot and bring to a boil. Simmer, covered, for 10 to 15 minutes, or until it smells strongly of ginger and is pale yellow. Remove from the heat and cool, with the lid on, until room temperature.

Pour the ginger tea into a large non-metal bowl with a spout or any other non-metal bowl. Pour the ginger bug through a fine strainer into the tea, add the lemon juice, and gently stir with a wooden spoon.

Pour the apple juice into the clean bottle, then top with the ginger tea mixture. Seal and set in a dark place for 3 to 10 days (see note). The timing is a wide range because temperature will play a large role. Pop (or burp) the bottle once a day to release any pressure buildup. After the ginger beer is very fizzy, the bottle is ready to refrigerate and drink. Store in the refrigerator for up to 2 weeks.

recipe continues . . .

ginger bug

NOTES

*A ginger bug can stay dormant in the refrigerator for months. The longest
I've kept it is about 4 months; I then fed it once and it was back in action the
next day. If you want to keep it for a while without using, cover it with a lid
or something non-permeable.*

*If your house is very hot, try to find a cool place for the ginger beer when it's
fermenting. The summer I wrote this book, I had a few bottles on the counter
and one exploded after less than 2 days, even though I had burped it earlier
that day. It was a record-breaking summer for heat, over 105°F (40°C), and
as I mentioned before, Dutch houses are not built for heat! I've read that
some people store their bottles in bins so that any explosions don't hurt
anyone nearby.*

Kombucha, Three Ways

Makes 1 gallon (4 litres) | 30 minutes prep time |
7 to 10 days fermenting time

*Kombucha is a bit more
complicated than ginger beer, at
least in that you have to get your
hands on a scoby, but I've had
good success with it even when
I've made mistakes. I'm laying
out instructions using black tea
because it's a bit easier for
beginners, but I often use green
tea instead. Like ginger beer,
sugar is used here, with juice or
fruit for the second ferment. This
part is optional if you don't care
for carbonation, but I encourage
a second ferment. You can buy a
scoby, or kombucha mushroom,
online from a number of websites,
or ask someone you know who
makes kombucha. Eventually,
you start swimming in them.
(Blend up extras and add them to
your compost or mix them with
the soil around acid-loving
plants.) The two flavours here are
made with half a batch of the
basic black kombucha. They can
easily be doubled, but I usually
like to keep a couple of plain
bottles and a couple of flavoured.*

Materials Needed

A large 1-gallon (4-litre) glass
   jar
Four 2-pint (1-litre) flip-top
   bottles

Basic Black

1 gallon (4 litres) water
4 tablespoons black tea, or
   6 tea bags
1 cup (200 grams) cane sugar
1 cup (250 ml) plain
   kombucha, from a previous
   batch or store-bought
1 scoby
3 cups (750 ml) apple juice

Strawberry Ginger

1 cup (200 grams)
   strawberries, hulled (and
   sliced if large)
1 tablespoon finely grated
   fresh ginger

Cranberry Citrus

½ cup (80 grams) fresh or
   dried cranberries
Zest of 1 orange
Zest of 1 lemon

To make the kombucha, first brew the tea. Boil the water and steep the
tea for 15 to 20 minutes in a large heatproof bowl. I usually place the
tea in a fine-mesh sieve to steep as it's too much for a regular infuser.

Add the sugar to the hot tea and whisk to dissolve. Cool to room
temperature.

Pour the cooled tea into a large jar or other non-metal container.
Add the kombucha, stir with a wooden spoon, then wash your hands
and place the scoby in the tea. Cover with a tea towel or other
densely woven material (to keep fruit flies out) and secure with an
elastic or string.

Place the fermenting kombucha in a dark, cool, low-traffic area of the
house, but one that doesn't have stale air (not a cellar). Don't move it
for a full 7 days.

recipe continues . . .

After the week is up, a new scoby should have formed, and you might see some spooky floating bits hanging out. All normal. There should also be some bubbling action. Taste your kombucha and check for your preference of sweetness and acidity. If you want it to be more acidic, leave it for a couple more days. Sweetness can be adjusted during the second fermentation. Taste daily.

Once the kombucha is to your taste, it's time to bottle for the second fermentation. Before using them, sanitize your bottles with boiling water or by running through the dishwasher. Remove the scoby(s) (see note) and reserve a cup of the kombucha for your next batch.

Split the apple juice equally between the four bottles, then top with the brewed kombucha. Place the bottles in a dark place at about 68°F (20°C) for 2 to 3 days, popping or burping daily to release any built-up pressure, until it's carbonated enough for your liking.

To make the strawberry ginger version, follow the recipe up until bottling (steps 1 to 6). Split the berries and ginger between two bottles, then fill with the fermented kombucha. Seal and keep in a dark place for 2 to 3 days, until very bubbly, burping daily. Strain when serving if you prefer.

To make the cranberry citrus version, follow the recipe up until bottling (steps 1 to 6). Place the cranberries and citrus zests in two bottles, then fill with the fermented kombucha. Seal and keep in a dark place for 2 to 3 days, until very bubbly, burping daily. Strain when serving if you prefer.

NOTE
Keep any extra scobys in the refrigerator in a sealed jar, with enough kombucha to cover, plus the reserved cup for your next batch. They'll last a few months this way, but not indefinitely.

Sourdough Starter

5 minutes prep time | 7 to 10 days fermenting time

My sourdough starter works well and creates well-risen loaves of bread. It's not as exact as many recipes, being a little more relaxed with measurements, but it does the trick. I prefer rye flour, as it creates an active starter more quickly than other types of flour, such as all-purpose, and is a beginner-friendly option.

For Each Feeding

2 tablespoons whole grain rye flour

2 tablespoons water

Mix the flour and water with a wooden spoon in a large (at least 17 ounces / 500 ml) glass jar. Cover with a tightly woven cloth and secure with an elastic band or set a lid on top without screwing it on.

For the next 7 to 10 days, feed your starter daily with the same amount of flour and water. Try to feed it at around the same time each day. You will likely see significant bubbling action after the first day or two, but this is a beginning surge and will die down. Don't be worried at this point! Regular feeding over the next few days will ensure a good, strong starter.

After day 3, discard extra starter if needed to keep the jar from overfilling. There's no need to be too picky about this; just scoop some out and toss it into the compost. Leave about 3 tablespoons of starter at the bottom of the jar (leave about this much every time you discard or use the starter). Every time you feed your starter going forward, you'll want to discard any extra if you're not using it for baking. If you feed a starter without discarding, you're more likely to over-ferment and end up with alcohol at the top of the jar.

Once about a week has passed, you should have a starter that rises and falls daily, over the course of several hours, with each feeding. If you're interested in seeing the growth of your starter, place an elastic band around the jar at the point the starter reaches when you feed it, which will provide a marker to compare the change. Your starter should be very active before you use it. If mould starts growing on it, toss the whole thing. If you forget to feed at the usual time one day, just feed it a bit later.

After the starter has reached its full potential (consistently rising significantly with each feeding), it will still need daily feeding or refrigeration. If you're not using it at least once a week, store it in the refrigerator. When you're ready to make your sourdough bread, simply remove from the refrigerator, feed the starter again, and use it the following day.

recipe continues . . .

NOTES

Some chemicals added to water can affect the growth of your starter. If you live in an area with high levels of chlorine in the water, leave the water you want to use for your starter on the counter, uncovered, for 24 hours beforehand. The chlorine will largely dissipate.

If you really want to be more exact, use 1 ounce (30 grams) of flour and 1 ounce (30 grams) of water for each feeding.

Once your starter is very active, you can use the discard for any number of recipes. You can see Baked The Blog, *a Canadian blogging collective I'm part of, for many sourdough discard recipes.*

Basic Spelt Sourdough

Makes one large loaf | 40 minutes prep time | 13 to 17 hours rising time | 50 minutes cooking time

I make this sourdough more often than any other bread, baking a loaf at least once a week. It's extraordinarily simple; there is a bit of stretching and folding, which the dark rye doesn't need, but that small extra effort makes a real difference. I almost exclusively make this with whole grain spelt, but using all light spelt or half and half results in a lovely light loaf. Whole grain will give you what you see pictured—a thin, crisp crust, a tighter crumb perfect for toppings that won't drip through, and out-of-this-world flavour.

3¾ cups (550 grams) spelt flour

1½ cups (375 ml) water, room temperature

¼ cup (50 grams) active Sourdough Starter (page 221, see note)

2 teaspoons (10 grams) salt

Add the flour, water, starter, and salt to a large bowl and stir well with a wooden spoon, until the dough is uniform and no streaks of flour remain. Cover with a tea towel.

Three times over the next half hour, once every 10 minutes, stretch and fold the dough. Flour your hands well and sprinkle some flour over the dough. Lift it in both hands and gently pull out to both sides, until about double the width, then fold over once. Turn the dough a quarter circle and pull the other direction, fold again, then set back in the bowl. Repeat twice with the break in between.

Once you're finished stretching the dough, it's ready to rest and rise. Set it in a draft-free place, covered with a tea towel and a plate. Let it rise for 12 hours, or up to 16 hours. The dough should approximately double in size.

Line a large, shallow bowl with a square of parchment paper and set aside. Alternatively, use a banneton if you have one.

After the dough has risen, generously flour a flat work surface. Place the dough on the floured surface, then stretch and rotate to create tension in the loaf. To do this, stretch a small portion of dough away from you, then fold back to the centre and allow it to stick to the dough. Rotate slightly and repeat, until a fairly tight ball has formed. This should take about 5 minutes.

Flip the dough over into the paper-lined bowl, cover with a tea towel, and set aside to rise for another hour.

Halfway through the second rise, preheat the oven. Set a covered round baking dish or Dutch oven with a lid, the largest you have, into your oven and preheat to 450°F (230°C).

recipe continues . . .

After about 15 minutes, once the baking dish is very hot, carefully remove the dish from the oven. Lift the parchment paper at the edges and place the dough in the dish, cover, and bake for 30 minutes. Remove the lid and bake for another 15 to 20 minutes, or until the dough is a dark golden colour.

Remove the bread from the pot and set on a cooling rack. After about 10 minutes, remove the paper and let the bread cool fully before slicing. I know you want warm bread, but this is an important step and will prevent your loaf from becoming gummy and producing dough lint. This bread stores well for up to 4 days. To keep the crispy crust, wrap the cut end in beeswax wrap or something similar and the rest of the loaf in a tea towel.

NOTE

Substitute ¼ teaspoon dry yeast or a pea-sized piece of fresh yeast for the starter if you prefer.

Scandinavian Dark Rye

Makes one loaf | 5 minutes prep time | 14 hours rising time |
45 minutes cooking time

This is a more deeply flavoured loaf than the basic spelt, which is already nutty and complex, with the addition of floral rye, cocoa, and oats. If you grew up in northern or eastern Europe, this bread will be very familiar to you. It's dark and dense, the type of bread I hated as a child but love now. If all you've ever had is the rectangular loaf that comes in paper-thin slices in that fitted plastic bag, this is not that.

2 cups (300 grams) spelt flour

1½ cups (200 grams) rye flour

½ cup (55 grams) rolled oats

¼ cup (25 grams) cocoa powder

1½ cups (375 ml) water, room temperature

¼ cup (50 grams) Sourdough Starter (page 221, see note)

2 teaspoons (10 grams) salt

Add the spelt flour, rye flour, oats, cocoa powder, water, starter, and salt to a large bowl and mix until well combined. The dough will be a bit shaggy. Cover with a tea towel and a plate, and set in a draft-free place for about 12 hours.

After 12 hours, the dough should be about double in size. Line a standard loaf tin (around 10 inches / 25 cm long) with parchment paper and place the dough in the tin. Cover again, using a dampened tea towel, and set aside to rise for another hour or so, up to 2 hours. The dough should almost double again in size during this time.

Preheat the oven to 400°F (200°C). Bake the bread for 40 to 45 minutes, or until the bread is a darker brown and probably has a cracked-open top.

Cool on a rack for 10 minutes before removing from the tin and cooling fully on the rack before slicing. This bread will last for about 5 days at room temperature, with the cut end covered in beeswax wrap and the whole loaf wrapped in a tea towel. This bread freezes very well, simply cooled fully and then frozen in a sealed container for up to a month. If you'd like, it can be sliced before freezing if you want just one or two slices a day.

NOTE
If you don't have a sourdough starter or don't want to make one, substitute ¼ teaspoon dry yeast or a pea-sized piece of fresh yeast for the starter.

Coconut Yogurt

Makes about 2 cups (500 ml) | 5 minutes prep time |
5 minutes cooking time | 24 hours fermenting time

Coconut yogurt is the easiest and best dairy-free yogurt to make at home. Simple, creamy, no yogurt maker required. This one is a bit lighter than some, good for muesli or simply with fruit, but also for savoury uses, as there's no sweetener added. I love it in summer with fresh berries. I had little success with using probiotic capsules to ferment, so I started my first batch with a bit of store-bought yogurt. After the first time, you can carry a few tablespoons over from your previous batch to ferment the new one. It's much more reliable this way.

1 can (13½ ounces / 400 ml) full-fat coconut milk
4 teaspoons tapioca starch (see note)
3 tablespoons coconut milk yogurt

Add the coconut milk to a small saucepan and heat over medium-low heat to bring to a simmer. Place the tapioca starch in a small bowl, then take ¼ cup (60 ml) of the hot coconut milk and whisk it into the starch to blend. Remove the pot from the heat and whisk in the tapioca starch mixture.

Cool the coconut milk mixture to about room temperature, then stir in the coconut milk yogurt. If there are any visible lumps, press the yogurt through a fine-mesh sieve. Place in a large glass jar or container and cover with a loose lid or tightly woven cloth, securing with an elastic band.

Place the yogurt mixture in a warm, dark place for 24 hours. An oven is ideal, but I often simply leave the jar on the counter. If you leave it at room temperature, it may need a little more time, an extra 2 to 4 hours or so. Check for tang or sourness after the 24 hours is up, then refrigerate for up to 1 week. Chill before eating.

NOTES

To make extra-thick coconut yogurt, use only the cream from a can of coconut milk, or use canned coconut cream. This thicker, ultra-rich version is best for topping desserts, like A Real Holiday Stunner (page 208), but is a little too much for every day. For a regular yogurt, stick with the full can of milk.

I tried and tried to make this recipe without tapioca starch, but it was awful every time. Without, it just turns into tangier coconut cream and goes rock hard in the refrigerator.

Occasionally Eggs

Coconut Labneh

Makes about 1½ cups (250 grams) | 5 minutes prep time |
12 to 16 hours chilling time

*Labneh is nothing more than
yogurt, strained until thick.
Coconut labneh is a bit sweet,
though not particularly so, and
can be added to both sweet and
savoury dishes. It makes an
appearance in a number of
recipes in this book. This is a
recipe I go back to again and
again; labneh adds a rare
richness to plant-based dishes
that's otherwise often lacking.
Coconut yogurt is ideal for
making a dairy-free labneh, as
it's thick to begin with—in my
experience, it doesn't really work
with nut- or oat-based yogurts.*

1 batch Coconut Yogurt (page 228) or 1 container (13½ ounces /
   400 ml) store-bought
Juice of ½ lemon
Pinch salt

Line a fine-mesh sieve with a tea towel or nut milk bag, and place
over a large bowl. In a smaller bowl, mix the yogurt, lemon juice,
and salt, then pour into the lined sieve. Twist and secure tightly so
that the yogurt resembles a disc, then refrigerate, still in the bowl,
for 12 to 16 hours.

After the yogurt has been sitting, there should be a significant quantity
of water in the bowl, and the resulting labneh should be very thick.
Scoop it out into a container, discarding the water, and refrigerate for
up to 3 days.

NOTE
*A nut milk bag is ideal for this recipe, but I don't have one, so I always use a
tea towel. Layered cheesecloth can also be used.*

Sauerkraut, Three Ways

Each recipe makes about 2 cups (400 grams) | 15 minutes prep time |
3 to 7 days fermenting time

NOTE

Pop-top glass jars are ideal for this recipe. To sterilize, run them through the dishwasher or boil for several minutes in a large pot of water.

It's surprising how easy it is to make good sauerkraut at home. Not the disappointing kind that comes in a bag, but a deliciously tangy, sour, crunchy version. There are three very different recipes here: a dill and mustard version that's reminiscent of a good sour pickle, a spicy turmeric golden kraut, and a jewel-toned sweet red with a kick of ginger.

Dill Pickle Sauerkraut

14 ounces (400 grams) green cabbage

¼ cup (15 grams) packed dill, dill heads reserved
  if available

1 teaspoon Dijon mustard

1 clove garlic, minced

2 teaspoons salt

2 to 3 dill heads, if possible

Take off the outer leaves of the cabbage, and core. Reserve one cabbage leaf. Finely chop the cabbage and add it to a large bowl with the dill, mustard, garlic, and salt.

Use your hands to massage the cabbage for about 10 minutes, until there is a significant amount of liquid (brine) in the bowl.

Sterilize a 17-ounce (500 ml) jar with a glass lid (see note) and place the dill heads in the base of the jar. Pack with the sauerkraut, making sure it's fully covered with the brine released during the massaging, then cover with a folded cabbage leaf and close the jar.

Set the jar into a bowl, then ferment for 3 to 7 days, tasting for acidity daily after day 3. Pop the jar daily to release excess pressure. Once it's to your taste, refrigerate for up to 3 months.

Spicy Orange Sauerkraut

14 ounces (400 grams) green cabbage

1 medium carrot

1 tablespoon grated fresh ginger

½ teaspoon ground turmeric (or 1 piece fresh,
  grated)

½ teaspoon cumin seeds

2 teaspoons salt

Remove the outer cabbage leaves and core, reserving one leaf. Grate or finely chop the cabbage and coarsely grate the carrot. Finely grate the ginger, leaving the skin on (and turmeric if using fresh).

Place the cabbage, carrot, ginger, turmeric, cumin, and salt in a large bowl and use your hands to massage for about 10 minutes, or until a large amount of liquid (brine) has released from the mixture.

Sterilize a 17-ounce (500 ml) jar with a glass lid (see note), and pack the sauerkraut into it, making sure it's fully covered by the brine. Cover with the folded cabbage leaf and close the jar.

Place the jar into a bowl, then set aside to ferment for 3 to 7 days, tasting daily after the 3-day mark for your preferred acidity or sourness. Pop daily to let excess pressure escape. Once it's sour enough, refrigerate for up to 6 months.

Classic Red Sauerkraut

14 ounces (400 grams) red cabbage

1 small beet

1 small apple

1 tablespoon grated fresh ginger

2 teaspoons salt

Remove the outer leaves and core of the cabbage, setting one leaf aside to use later. Coarsely grate or finely chop the cabbage. Peel the beet and core the apple, and grate both. Finely grate the ginger, leaving the skin on.

Place the cabbage, beet, apple, ginger, and salt in a large bowl and use your hands to massage for about 10 minutes, or until a large amount of liquid (brine) has released from the cabbage.

Sterilize a 17-ounce (500 ml) jar with a glass lid (see note), and pack the sauerkraut into the jar, pressing firmly. Everything should be fully covered with brine. Fold the reserved cabbage leaf and place it over the kraut, then seal and place the jar in a bowl.

Let the sauerkraut ferment for 3 to 7 days, tasting daily after the third day. Pop the lid daily to release excess pressure. Once it's completed fermenting—when it's sour enough to your liking—store in the refrigerator for up to 6 months.

Staples

These are my staples, my go-to recipes that I think everyone should be able to make if interested in whole food cooking. Homemade milk, basic vinaigrettes, pickled onions, vegetable stock—some of these are things I've been making for over twenty years, and some only since I started eating vegetarian. I switched from chicken stock to veg, for example, and obviously haven't always made my own milk.

You may not use all of these recipes, but they are used throughout the book. They often provide the backbone to a recipe or lift it up into something much better. They might be useful for preserving a garden bounty or are simply basic recipes that are good knowledge to have, far beyond the covers of this cookbook.

Some of these are made at home because it's much less expensive, some to avoid too much packaging and plastic, and others just because they're fun or useful to have around. Milk, for example, isn't much different from the store-bought version, but those tetra containers build up quickly—and depending on where you live, the non-dairy milk available to buy might be filled with additives, thickeners, and sweeteners.

All of these recipes can be made with the basic equipment laid out earlier in the book. None of the milks needs a high-speed blender, and you won't need a gargantuan stockpot, or a standing mixer, or even a food processor.

In addition to reducing your use of plastic and other packaging, homemade is often more budget-friendly than store-bought. It becomes habit after some time, and there is a sense of independence and freedom that comes from making these staples at home instead of buying them.

Plant Milks and Creams

I had planned to do an all-encompassing guideline for making plant milks, but ended up with the three that can be most easily made without a high-speed blender. I make these with an immersion blender and they always work well. Oat is my go-to, with a couple of batches every week, since cashews and hemp are rather more expensive. It's nice to have a cream in the refrigerator for a variety of uses, and if you run out of milk for a smoothie, you can thin out a bit of cream and use it instead.

GF | NF | SF

After several years of homemade oat milk, I've come to the conclusion that a nut milk bag should be avoided. It's part of what causes the dreaded slime. Using a fine-mesh sieve instead makes a fairly creamy milk with a good texture. Oat milk is so easy and cheap to make, and I find this holds up to any store-bought stuff I've tried.

Oat Milk

Makes 4 cups (1 litre) | 5 minutes prep time | 2 hours soaking time

1 cup (110 grams) rolled oats
1 litre (4 cups) water

Soak the oats in hot water for about 2 hours.

After soaking, drain and rinse the oats in a fine-mesh sieve. Add to a blender with the water and mix on low until creamy, or use a large container and an immersion blender on high speed.

Once the oats are blended, drain the milk through a fine-mesh sieve, using a spoon to move the oat pulp around to release all the milk. Pour the milk into a bottle and refrigerate for up to 1 week.

GF | NF

Oat cream is a revelation. I had been occasionally buying it, but the packaged ones all use palm oil and a few other questionable ingredients. Homemade is simpler, is (much) cheaper, and doesn't involve plastic. Some of my favourite ways to use it are in the Winter Vegetable Pot Pie (page 195) or stirred into tomato sauce, soups, or a quick garlic pasta. Only add the maple syrup if you're going to be using this for something sweet.

Oat Cream

Makes about 2 cups (500 ml) | 5 minutes prep time | 2 hours soaking time

1½ cups (165 grams) rolled oats
2 cups (500 ml) water
2 tablespoons grapeseed oil
Pinch salt
1 teaspoon maple syrup or honey (optional)

Soak the oats in hot water for about 2 hours. Rinse through a fine-mesh sieve, then add them to a blender with the water, oil, salt, and maple syrup, if using. Mix on low until very smooth. Alternatively, use a large container and an immersion blender.

recipe continues . . .

Once blended, drain through a fine-mesh sieve and use a spoon to move the oat pulp around to allow the cream through. Pour into a jar and refrigerate for up to 1 week.

NOTES

Keep in mind that homemade oat milk and cream tend to thicken when heated, and they're often not the best choice for hot drinks or to use in cream sauces—though they're fine as an addition to sauces like tomato.

A very high-powered blender, like a Vitamix, is not your friend here. You must have some pulp remaining at the end of blending or the milk/cream will be slimy.

GF | SF

Cashew is arguably the most luxurious of all plant milks, creamy and slightly sweet. I stretch it a bit with a little more water than usual, which doesn't make much of a difference, and it's the best in any milk-based drinks, like hot chocolate. There are a couple of recipes on my website using cashew pulp, if you want to make use of it.

Cashew Milk
Makes about 3½ cups (875 ml) | 5 minutes prep time | 1 hour soaking time

1 cup (150 grams) cashews
3½ cups (875 ml) water

Soak the cashews for at least 1 hour in very hot water, or overnight. Rinse well. Add to a blender with the water and mix on high speed until creamy, or use an immersion blender in a large bowl.

Drain the milk using a fine-mesh sieve or a nut milk bag. Store the milk for up to a week in a sealed bottle or jar. The pulp can be used in cookies or granola bars, added to bread, and so on.

GF

Like the milk, cashew cream is deluxe. I rarely make this—it's more for holidays or special occasions—but it's really something. Cashew cream makes an excellent ice cream base, glaze for cakes, or topping for fruit. I personally don't like it in savoury recipes—cashews are naturally too sweet. I usually add a little vanilla and honey or maple syrup to exaggerate the sweetness further for use in desserts.

Cashew Cream
Makes about 1 cup | 5 minutes prep time | 2 hours soaking time

1 cup (150 grams) cashews
¾ cup (180 ml) water
2 teaspoons honey (optional)
½ teaspoon vanilla extract (optional)

Soak the cashews in hot water for at least 2 hours, or overnight. Rinse well. Add to a blender with the water and the honey and vanilla (if using), and blend on high until very smooth and creamy. Alternatively, use an immersion blender in a large container.

Don't strain the cream. Store in a jar or sealed container in the refrigerator for up to 1 week.

A lot of hemp is grown in Manitoba, and in northern Europe we often see hemp that's imported from Canada. This milk has a stronger flavour than the cashew and oat milks— noticeably hemp-like, very nutty—but not in a bad way. The great thing is, it isn't necessary to soak the hemp, even when using an immersion blender. Hemp pulp can be used in the same way as cashew or any other nut pulp.

Hemp Milk

Makes 4 cups (1 litre) | 5 minutes prep time

4 cups (1 litre) water
½ cup (80 grams) hemp hearts

Place the water and hemp in a blender and mix on high speed until smooth, or blend with an immersion blender in a large container.

Drain the milk through a nut milk bag or fine-mesh sieve, using a spoon to move the hemp pulp to release the milk. Store in the refrigerator for up to 1 week in a sealed jar or bottle.

Hemp cream is also great to use in savoury cooking, much like oat. I wouldn't recommend it in tea or coffee, but it's excellent in a stew. This has the consistency of half and half cream, but you can reduce the water to make it into a thicker cream. Unlike the milk, the hemp is soaked for cream as it results in a richer texture and breaks down more easily.

Hemp Cream

Makes about 2 cups (500 ml) | 5 minutes prep time | 1 hour soaking time

½ cup (80 grams) hemp hearts
2 cups (500 ml) water
Pinch salt

Soak the hemp in hot water for at least 1 hour. Drain through a fine-mesh sieve and rinse well, then add to a blender with the water and salt and mix on high speed until very creamy. Alternatively, use an immersion blender in a deep container.

Pour the cream through a fine-mesh sieve into a jar or container and refrigerate for up to 1 week.

NOTE

For those curious, you can also make milk from sesame, pumpkin, and sunflower seeds, with a one part seeds to three parts water ratio. Almond, hazelnut, and other nuts are one part nuts to four parts water. All should be soaked overnight first. Coconut milk always hardens in the refrigerator, so I don't make it.

Nut and Seed Butter

Makes about 2 cups (400 grams) | 5 minutes prep time |
15 minutes cooking time | 10 minutes blending time

*My general preference for a nut
and seed butter is for mostly
sunflower seeds with about one-
quarter hazelnuts and walnuts
mixed in. Any blend is good—
sesame seeds, pumpkin seeds
(they will result in a greenish
tinge if you use too much),
cashews, almonds, and so on.
Hemp is nice but can't be roasted,
so add it just before blending if
you'd like to use it. You don't
need a fancy food processor for
this recipe—mine is one of the
cheapest on the market—but you
will need a good bit of time to
blend, and blending time will be
even longer with a lower-end
processor.*

2½ cups (400 grams) mixed nuts and seeds

½ teaspoon salt

1 to 2 soft dates, pitted (optional, see note)

Preheat the oven to 300°F (150°C). Roast the seeds and nuts on a large
baking sheet for about 15 minutes, or until golden and shining.

Cool for 15 minutes, then add to a food processor with the salt and
dates (if using). Blend on high speed for about 10 minutes, scraping
down the sides as needed. The butter should be very, very smooth,
glossy, and liquid in appearance when ready. When you think it's
done, blend for another minute.

Store the butter in a jar or sealed container in the refrigerator for up
to a month. I can usually keep mine on the counter for up to a week
because we go through it so quickly (also because I have a tiny
European refrigerator).

NOTE
*Coconut sugar can be used instead of dates, but a liquid sweetener, like
maple syrup or honey, will cause the butter to seize.*

Vegetable Stock

Makes 1 gallon (4 litres) | 10 minutes prep time | 1 hour cooking time

Although I've listed the ingredients as fresh, what I more often do is make this stock with vegetable scraps mixed with fresh. Carrot ends, leek tops, parsley stems, celery leaves, mushroom stalks—the food that we waste is endless. If you want to do this, make sure to keep scraps from the vegetables listed here and not any old veg. I keep my scraps for a few days, in a container either in the refrigerator door or the freezer, then mix with whatever fresh is needed to top it off and go with that. Homemade vegetable stock is excellent, and much better than powdered (though I keep powdered stock in the house, too, to use in a pinch).

1 gallon (4 litres) water

3 stalks celery

2 leeks

2 carrots

2 yellow onions

2 cups (200 grams) button mushrooms

4 cloves garlic

½ cup (30 grams) parsley

A few sprigs thyme

6 peppercorns

3 bay leaves

1 tablespoon salt

Add the water to a large pot. Coarsely chop the celery, leeks, carrots, onions, and mushrooms.

Add the chopped vegetables, garlic, parsley, thyme, peppercorns, bay leaves, and salt to the pot. Over high heat, bring to a rolling boil, then reduce the heat and simmer, covered, for 50 to 60 minutes. The stock should be a pleasant golden colour when it's finished.

Strain the stock, then taste and season as needed. If you want it as broth for drinking, make sure it's well seasoned. If it's for soup, don't worry about it too much, as salt and other seasonings can be added later.

Freeze for up to 6 months, or refrigerate for up to a week. I usually freeze in 2-pint (1-litre) jars for making soup. If freezing, make sure to leave some space at the top of the jar, as the stock will expand as it freezes.

NOTES

To quickly clean leeks, slice them lengthwise without cutting all the way through. Rinse them under running water, using your hands to open up the layers to remove any dirt and sand.

There's no need to separate the leaves from the stems of herbs for this recipe. Just toss them all in.

Harissa

Makes about ½ cup (125 ml) | 10 minutes prep time | 15 minutes cooking time

2 tablespoons olive oil

½ red onion, sliced

1 red bell pepper, seeded and sliced

1 jalapeño pepper, chopped

3 cloves garlic, chopped

2 teaspoons cumin seeds

1 teaspoon coriander seeds

½ teaspoon salt

1 plum tomato, chopped

Juice of 1 lemon

Add the oil, onions, bell peppers, and jalapeños to a large frying pan and cook over low heat, stirring often, for about 10 minutes, until softened.

Stir in the garlic, cumin, coriander, and salt, then add the tomatoes. Cook for another 5 minutes, stirring. Remove from the heat and add the lemon juice. Use an immersion blender to purée into a rough paste, and store in a sealed container in the refrigerator for up to 1 week. Alternatively, you can use a small standing blender or food processor to blend, but cool the mixture beforehand.

Chermoula

Makes about ½ cup (125 ml) | 5 minutes prep time

1 cup (60 grams) parsley and cilantro (in whatever ratio you wish)

¼ cup (15 grams) oregano leaves

3 cloves garlic

Zest of 1 lemon

Juice of 1 lemon

½ teaspoon finely grated fresh ginger

½ teaspoon salt

½ teaspoon cumin seeds

½ teaspoon coriander seeds

½ teaspoon cayenne pepper

½ cup (125 ml) olive oil

Add the parsley, cilantro, oregano, garlic, lemon zest, lemon juice, ginger, salt, cumin, coriander, cayenne, and oil to a food processor and blend until fairly smooth but with a loose consistency. Alternatively, use a deep container and an immersion blender. This can be stored for a couple of days in a sealed container in the refrigerator, or frozen in the same way as the Herbs in Oil (page 255).

Basic Tahini Dressing

Makes about ½ cup (125 ml) | 5 minutes prep time

*My go-to for roasted vegetables,
grain bowls, and falafel! This is a
great standard to have in your
repertoire. Some types of tahini
can be temperamental and may
thicken into a singular mass in
this dressing. Should that
happen, simply thin with a little
water and mix again. This
dressing tends to thicken slightly
as it stands, in any case. If you
don't have lemons, a couple of
tablespoons of apple cider vinegar
do just as well.*

3 tablespoons olive oil

3 tablespoons tahini

Juice of ½ lemon

1 clove garlic, minced

½ teaspoon honey

¼ teaspoon salt

¼ teaspoon freshly ground pepper

Water to thin, if needed

Add the oil, tahini, lemon juice, garlic, honey, salt, and pepper to a jar
or other container and mix until combined. Add a splash of water if
needed to thin. Use immediately or refrigerate in a sealed container
for up to 1 week.

Simple Dijon Vinaigrette

Makes enough for one large salad | 5 minutes prep time

*We never had store-bought salad
dressing in the house when I was
growing up, and my mom always
asked my older sister or me to
make the salad dressing. I used
to go way overboard with the
vinegar, but have managed to
find a good balance in the twenty
years since. I prefer balsamic
vinegar, either red or white, in
this and usually use the full
3 tablespoons. If you instead use
a more acidic vinegar, like apple
cider, go with 2 tablespoons. This
is what I make for virtually every
salad I toss together from what's
in the garden, and I like to make
a double batch to keep in the
refrigerator for the week.*

¼ cup (60 ml) olive oil

2 to 3 tablespoons balsamic vinegar

½ teaspoon honey

½ teaspoon Dijon mustard

¼ teaspoon salt

¼ teaspoon freshly ground pepper

Add the oil, vinegar, honey, mustard, salt, and pepper to a bowl or jar
and mix well to combine. It should be fully emulsified with no
separation of oil. Use immediately or refrigerate for up to 1 week. If
refrigerated, the oil will likely harden. Simply set it out at room
temperature for a few minutes and mix again.

A Moroccan spice blend isn't that much different from a curry blend—they use many of the same spices, just in different quantities. Cinnamon is a telltale element of Moroccan cooking and is often used liberally. If you haven't had cinnamon in savoury food before, you should try it—it's excellent. Whole spices are used when possible here, but feel free to substitute ground if needed.

Moroccan Spice Blend

Makes about ¼ cup (20 grams) | 5 minutes prep time | 1 minute cooking time

1 tablespoon cumin seeds

1 tablespoon cinnamon

1 tablespoon paprika

2 teaspoons freshly ground pepper

2 teaspoons dried ginger (see note)

1 teaspoon coriander seeds

1 teaspoon cayenne pepper

Toast the cumin, cinnamon, paprika, pepper, ginger, coriander, and cayenne in a pan over medium heat for about 30 seconds, stirring frequently to prevent burning. Remove from the pan and grind, using a clean coffee grinder or mortar and pestle. Store for up to 3 months in a sealed container.

I have an Indian spice box, or masala dabba, that Asha Shivakumar sent me when her first book was published. So honestly, I keep that on hand with fresh spices more often than I make this blend to store, but this is the mix that I most often add to curries. Putting it together is very convenient and it makes a nice addition to your spice drawer. I've omitted ginger from this, as I far prefer to use fresh ginger. If you want to, add a teaspoon of dried ginger to the mix.

Curry Spice Blend

Makes about ¼ cup (20 grams) | 5 minutes prep time | 1 minute cooking time

1 tablespoon cumin seeds

1 tablespoon ground turmeric

1 tablespoon fenugreek seeds

1 teaspoon coriander seeds

1 teaspoon cayenne pepper

Seeds of 3 cardamom pods

½ teaspoon freshly ground pepper

½ teaspoon mustard seeds

Toast the cumin, turmeric, fenugreek, coriander, cayenne, cardamom, pepper, and mustard in a frying pan over medium heat for 20 to 30 seconds, stirring frequently. Grind in a clean coffee grinder or with a mortar and pestle, and store for up to 3 months in a sealed container.

NOTES

To clean a coffee grinder, wipe it out with a clean cloth and then grind a small amount of rice in it.

Dried ginger can sometimes be found in the spice section of the grocery store, or you can make it yourself by grating and air-drying fresh ginger. If you can't find it, use ground ginger.

Roasted Garlic, Two Ways

Makes one to four heads of garlic, or more | 5 minutes prep time |
20 to 60 minutes cooking time

There are two very good ways to roast garlic. For the first, you cut the tops off the cloves and keep the head intact, and then roast, squeezing the garlic out afterward. Very fun, looks cool. For this method, use at least four heads of garlic to make it worthwhile. The second is decidedly less exciting but probably more practical, since we don't often need a whole head of roasted garlic: single cloves are roasted with the skin on, then peeled and used. I use this method more often, but have a fondness for the first. If you want to go a lower-waste way, try the second method!

Method 1

4 heads garlic, or more
2 to 3 tablespoons olive oil

Preheat the oven to 400°F (200°C). Cut the tops off the whole heads of garlic. Place in a Dutch oven or lidded baking dish, drizzle with a little olive oil, and cover.

Roast for 50 to 60 minutes, until a deep golden brown. Remove from the oven, take the lid off, and carefully lift the heads out using tongs.

Cool until the garlic can be safely touched, then squeeze from the base up to release the roasted garlic cloves. Keep the roasted garlic in a sealed container, covered with more olive oil, in the refrigerator for up to 2 weeks. Alternatively, blend with a drizzle of olive oil and freeze in ice cube trays to add to soups, stews, and sauces. As this makes so much, sometimes I freeze the garlic (cloves should be removed from their skins beforehand) in a sealed container and take individual cloves as needed for cooking.

Method 2

1 head garlic
2 tablespoons olive oil

Preheat the oven to 400°F (200°C). Break a head of garlic into individual cloves and place on a baking sheet.

Drizzle with olive oil and roast for 20 to 25 minutes, or until golden brown. Remove from the oven. Once cool enough to touch, gently peel the cloves and remove the roasted garlic. This method is ideal for roasting a couple of cloves with other vegetables.

Keep the roasted garlic in a sealed container, covered with more olive oil, in the refrigerator for up to 2 weeks. Alternatively, blend with a drizzle of olive oil and freeze in ice cube trays to add to soups, stews, and sauces.

Caramelized Onions

Makes about 1½ cups (240 grams) | 10 minutes prep time |
1 hour cooking time

*Caramelized onions need a long
cooking time, and that's that. It's
just a fact. I can't count the
number of times I've seen people
talk about caramelizing onions
when they're just sweating them,
and I have to say, it really bothers
me—which, for me, means
gesturing at the screen and
shouting. So yes, they need an
hour. You can do other things
while they're cooking, and they
are unequivocally worth it.*

2 teaspoons olive oil

6 small yellow onions, thinly sliced

1 teaspoon salt

1 teaspoon freshly ground pepper

1 tablespoon balsamic vinegar

Add the oil, onions, salt, and pepper to a large frying pan and heat
over low heat. Cook for about 1 hour, stirring frequently, or until soft
and a dark golden colour. There will likely be some sugar sticking to
the bottom of the pan and the onions should smell and taste quite
sweet. They should not brown or crisp.

Once the onions have caramelized, stir in the vinegar to lift any sugars
that have stuck to the pan. Refrigerate for up to 5 days.

NOTE
*The sliced raw onions will be a shockingly large pile. They will reduce
significantly.*

Pickled Red Onions

Makes about ¾ cup (120 grams) | 10 minutes prep time |
1 hour resting time

*Pickled onions are popular
worldwide, in a huge number of
variations, but red onions have
two advantages. One, they're
sweeter than white onions, and
two, they're a beautiful, vibrant
pink hue after pickling. This is
an excellent condiment to keep
on hand, especially in the cooler
months when food tends to turn
a bit beige. Add them to the
Nordic Burgers (page 50), a Meso
Bowl (page 140), Curry Burgers
(page 199), tacos, grain bowls,
pitas, or anything that could
use a lift.*

2 red onions, thinly sliced

¼ teaspoon salt

¼ teaspoon honey

Juice of 1 lemon

Place the onions, salt, honey, and lemon juice in a jar or bowl and mix
well. Cover and let sit at room temperature for at least 1 hour, or until
the onions are a uniform pink colour throughout. These will keep,
refrigerated in a sealed container, for at least a week.

Herbs in Oil

Makes about 1 cup (250 ml) | 10 minutes prep time

This is one of the best ways to preserve summer, and ideal for adding to soups, stews, and grain or pasta dishes during the dark of winter. A cube of basil lifts minestrone, thyme adds depth to a warming stew, parsley brightens. The four herbs listed are the ones that I've found to be most effective—sage and rosemary, for example, don't do at all well here. My mom has always done this with basil just before the first frost hits, and it's so good to have in the freezer.

5 cups (300 grams) packed basil, oregano, parsley, or thyme (see note)
6 cloves garlic
Juice of 1 lemon
¹⁄₂ teaspoon salt
¹⁄₄ cup (60 ml) olive oil

Add the herbs of choice, garlic, lemon juice, and salt to a food processor and blend until very finely chopped. Pour in the olive oil in a slow stream while blending, until well mixed and homogeneous.

Either freeze the mixture in ice cube trays or line a baking sheet with parchment paper and freeze dollops instead. Store in the freezer in a sealed container for up to 6 months.

NOTE
Thyme leaves should always be removed from the woody stem. Since thyme has such tiny leaves, it is best combined with another green, like spinach, for this. In that case, use about 1 cup (20 grams) thyme and make up the difference with spinach or another hardy green.

Whipped Coconut Cream

Makes about 2 cups (500 ml) | 5 minutes prep time |
24 hours chilling time

*Coconut whipped cream has a
reputation for being difficult to
make, depending on the brand or
if any additives are in the milk.
Really, though, the only thing
you need to do is shake the can
before you buy it. You want the
cream to be separate from the
water. Hear it slosh? Ditch it. If it
doesn't seem to move at all inside
the can, you're good to go. This
can be used in place of dairy
whipped cream for almost any
recipe. It's fluffy, rich, and
satisfyingly creamy.*

1 can (13½ ounces / 400 ml) full-fat coconut milk

1 tablespoon honey, or to taste

½ teaspoon vanilla extract

Chill the can of coconut milk for at least 24 hours. If you know you're going to be making whipped cream often, keep a can at the back of the refrigerator.

Scoop the cream from the top of the can, leaving any remaining water behind. Add it to a large mixing bowl with the honey and vanilla, then whip at a high speed until soft peaks form.

The cream is best used immediately, or at least applied immediately, as it hardens quickly if refrigerated again.

NOTE

The coconut water can be used in smoothies like the Winter Green (page 200), for cooking rice, or to thin out curries and stews.

Why I Choose Organic

I grew up on a working farm in the Canadian Prairies and have seen some of the impacts of conventional farming first-hand. My family, friends, and neighbours were and are farmers using standard practices. They're not bad people. Like everyone else, farmers just want to support their families, and there's a system in place that encourages, sometimes forces, people to use conventional methods. And organic farming is much more difficult, especially if you want to be certified.

I'm not really sure when it became important to me to choose organic food when possible, but it was early enough that I chose to focus on it at university, so before I was seventeen. I studied organic food systems and the impacts of conventional agricultural practices, particularly how they affect the workers who are exposed to high levels of pesticides and herbicides.

When these issues are discussed, in my experience both in North America and Europe, the emphasis is often on whether the global population can subsist on organic agriculture. There are several peer-reviewed, ethically funded (in other words, not by agrochemical companies) articles showing solid research into this, and they suggest that it is certainly possible to feed the world through organic agriculture and horticulture.[1]

Simply switching the existing system to organic doesn't solve the larger issues. The system is the problem. There is still the high environmental impact of importing food to consider, eating out of season, consuming too many luxury foods in the Global North (avocados, looking at you), clear-cutting for cash crops, and consuming too much meat and other animal products.[2] Combined, partial implementation of practices such as reducing food waste, reducing animal production and consumption, and using arable land for human food production would provide a more sustainable future for food.

Right now, organic food is a luxury—yet when I ask farmers who use conventional methods why they do that, the answer is often to prevent malformed or damaged crops. In theory, that should mean that organic food, with all its defects, should be less expensive. The reality, of course, is that farming is like any other job and people want to make a living in a very difficult field of work. Pesticides help to provide some guarantee that a crop will be successful—a guarantee that's becoming more difficult as climate change wreaks havoc on the growing seasons, but with a wrenching irony, as conventional farming practices contribute to that change and otherwise further degrade the soil and water they're using to grow food.

Organic food is not an individual health choice, or at least it shouldn't be. If that's the perspective you're coming from, there are many other reasons to choose organic when possible. I had never really considered that it might be an issue of personal health until I saw another blogger talking about how she purposely chooses not to buy organic because she doesn't believe that it's healthier for her. That being said, cancer rates in farm workers who are exposed to high levels of conventional pesticides suggest that there may be a link to ongoing exposure and cancer or other illnesses. Regarding individual health, however, the most recent significant study on the topic shows that organic crops have significantly higher levels of antioxidants and much lower levels of toxic heavy metals and pesticide residues.[3]

For me, organic food is more about making the best choice I can for others, specifically those who work within the supply chain, and for the environment. Certified organic agriculture still has problems—monoculture, large-scale farms, the environmental cost of shipping food long distances, and more. But it's often the best option in a supermarket, and not everyone has access to local, organic, farm-fresh food, or their own garden. I don't follow the dirty dozen and clean fifteen because it's a very shallow concept of how to choose organic. Just because avocados don't have high levels of pesticides in the part that you eat doesn't mean they're not being sprayed as much as strawberries.

There are three main issues to consider when making food choices. Conditions for farm workers, the environmental impact, and eating seasonally and locally when possible, which also tie into environmental concerns. There's a brief discussion about the implications for mental health, too.

HOW IS ORGANIC DEFINED?

Organic is defined in a few different ways, depending on where you are. In the EU, an organic certification means fewer pesticides, with those used both heavily regulated in terms of type and application, and minimal usage. It also means that animals and animal products are "free range" (which doesn't necessarily mean what we think it means), that no artificial colours and preservatives can be used, that there's no routine use of antibiotics for animals, that there's no genetically modified ingredients, and that fertilizers must be from plant or animal sources (like seaweed or manure) as opposed to synthetic fertilizers. The EU also encourages organic farming through a number of incentives within the union.

In Canada, the government states that its practices are equal to those followed in Europe. In my experience, Canada is not as stringent, but if you trust the government, then there you are. In conventional farming in Canada, much of the solid human waste (read "poop/medications/drugs") from water treatment plants is used to fertilize fields.

The US Department of Agriculture specifies that "synthetic pesticides and fertilizers, sewage sludge, irradiation, and genetic engineering may not be used"[4] in organic farming. So that's reassuring. It's worth noting that all of those practices—and more—can be and are used in conventional farming in the US.

Non-certified organic is also a thing. In Canada, at least, the buffer zone needed is a big hindrance to organic certification, especially for smaller-scale farmers. The market farm I worked at for a couple of years, for example, wasn't certified because a nearby strawberry farm sprayed its crops heavily, so the market farm couldn't ensure that there was no pesticide drift. As a result, they were not permitted to market their product as organic, and if you're looking at buying local, it's going to be like that a lot of the time. The best way to find out about a farmer's growing practices is simply to ask, and most of the time farmers will be happy to tell you about what they do and use on their farms and fields. Some, especially market farmers and CSA (community supported agriculture) growers, are often happy to have customers out to visit their farms to see what's going on. Food doesn't need to be certified to be grown sustainably.

WORKING CONDITIONS

It doesn't matter where in the world these large supply chain farms are; in Central America, the US, Europe, Africa—it's virtually the same the world over. Some of the biggest issues are large-scale pesticide use affecting individual health, terrible working conditions, and true wage slavery. A lot of attention is given to the types of labour used for clothing items, or fast fashion, for example, but the food system works in the same way. Yes, there are children picking your supermarket tomatoes, and yes, they are suffering.

Pesticides and herbicides are often sprayed directly onto fields while people are working. This is generally done without any notice and with little education about how to behave around these sprays, meaning workers use little to no protection in the form of respiratory or skin barriers.[5] Women are often disproportionately affected by this, as they are not only working in the fields but also doing additional related work, such as washing contaminated clothing. In addition, women are often not considered to be pesticide users, and preventative measures such as hazard warnings are not distributed to them.[6]

In the early 1990s, severe cases of pesticide poisoning amounted to 3 million worldwide each year, with over 220,000 deaths as a direct result, and an additional 25 million systematic occupational poisonings occurring each year in agricultural workers.[7] It is likely that these numbers have increased over the past two decades. Pesticide poisoning can involve increased respiratory and skin problems, vomiting, abdominal pain, reproductive illness, thyroid disease, and more.[8]

Repeated long-term exposure has been associated with health problems such as cancer, both in workers and their children, reproductive defects, and behavioural changes in those with extended exposure.[9] Women are often forced to bring babies and small children to work with them, which has a direct impact on the infant mortality rate of farm workers in conventional agriculture.[10] This is not just happening in developing countries. Here in the Netherlands, it was found that women working in greenhouses growing conventionally produced flowers were four times as likely to miscarry during pregnancy.[11]

In the US and Canada, migrant workers are acutely affected by agrochemicals, as well as unethical employment practices. Temporary or seasonal farm workers from Mexico and Central American countries make up the bulk of workers all along the west coast, from California to British Columbia. They are often paid per pound picked, to skip over the local minimum wage requirements, and they often live in unsafe conditions provided by employers. If they don't reach their quota on any particular day, workers are usually immediately fired and ejected from the farm. Migrant workers also suffer from constant fear and anxiety due to temporary or undocumented status, especially in the US.[12]

Sustainable farming practices have been shown to result in improved conditions for workers through higher pay, little or no exposure to agrochemicals, and better working conditions in general.[13]

ENVIRONMENTAL IMPACTS

In the conversation about organic food, the environmental impact is more frequently discussed and a bigger talking point much of the time than, for example, the individual human impact. Monoculture, which is used for both conventional and organic farming, increases pest populations, and in turn, large amounts of agrochemicals are used to ensure the appearance of a high-quality end product.[14] This is part of what's driving the ugly food movement to try to get people to embrace food that isn't picture-perfect, because it tastes the same.

Livestock production is the largest use of land globally, with most of the environmental impacts coming from feed production.[15] My grandmother, along with a single mother, in postwar Germany lived on vegetables from the garden and potatoes they helped to harvest once a year, some eggs and dairy, and very infrequent meat. My mom grew up having meat once a week, and in small quantities. My parents now eat meat at least once or twice daily, with any vegetarian meals invariably including large amounts of dairy and/or eggs.

This is the new normal for many people in North America and Europe—by new, I mean postwar—and although there is an ongoing shift toward vegetarianism[15] and at least a part-time plant-based diet, I don't think it's plausible to tell everyone to simply give up all animal products altogether. I clearly don't follow a vegan diet, but it is what works for me. A vegan diet isn't the be-all and end-all for a sustainable diet—imported soy from the Amazon, which is then processed, packed in plastic, and shipped to multiple locations, is worse for the environment than the occasional egg. A simple reduction, even removing meat from the diet once a week, makes a significant difference.

So there are many different factors to consider. Are you eating a vegan diet with primarily imported, out-of-season foods? Or plant-based with a seasonal focus? Are you eating a diet with some animal products, but trying to buy locally? Are you trying to eat organic food for the most part, and shopping at your local market? There's nothing wrong with any of these diet choices—it should be what works best for you at this time.

IMPACTS ON MENTAL HEALTH

For me, the accessibility of variable diets and how they might affect mental health also need to be considered. A few years ago, I shifted from a very careful vegetarian diet to including some chicken and very occasional fish for a period because I was living with my parents, had severe mental illness, and was often unable to cook for myself for a number of reasons.

Trying to make my own food and eating separately from everyone else created a lot of problems, and making the choice to include some animal products was ultimately better for me when I was struggling with daily panic attacks and major depression with suicidal episodes and hallucinations. After moving into my own home, and then moving overseas, I cut meat and fish out of my diet again and haven't suffered any ill effects, though I'll be coping with major depression my whole life.

I think for children and young adults, or other people with little choice, however, a reduction might be the only possibility. Not everyone can buy local, or organic, or fresh food. Before my partner and I moved to Europe, we lived almost exclusively on potatoes and broccoli for vegetables because they were the only organic foods available outside markets in our small prairie city at that time. I have made many financial sacrifices to buy organic food, and I'm fine with that, but I also work from home and can wear pants with holes in them.

LOCAL FOOD

Eating locally ensures that you're eating within the seasons, and it's often easier to find food that has been grown sustainably at the local level (certified or not). You can usually find local food at farmers' markets or neighbourhood shops, and sometimes at bigger supermarkets. There's been more consumer interest lately in supermarkets having more product from local suppliers. Buying produce from a farmer's market is often cheaper than from the supermarket, if buying directly from the producer, despite popular opinion.

So how can you support a local farm? If you have the means to do so, shop at a farmer's market at least for produce, or for some of the produce you buy. Usually you can get all fruits and vegetables, eggs and other animal products, honey or maple syrup, bread and/or grains and flour, some nuts and seeds, and so on from local producers. It depends on what can be grown in your region.

Talk to sellers at markets and ask them about other ways you can receive produce from them. Look into CSAs, for example, to receive a food share or a box, usually once a week, with whatever was grown on the farm or plot that week. This is the coolest way to get seasonal, and often rare, produce that you may not be able to find in stores. Most farms that run both a CSA and do the market save their fun and less common stuff for the food share.

The other neat thing about a CSA is that it ensures longevity for the farmer, because they know that they'll make a certain amount of money that year right at the beginning of the season. Depending on where you are, this share might go on all year, but usually it's for part of the year. It's often a single payment at the beginning of the season, and it can be a bit tricky to swing that, but some places will let you pay in instalments.

Unlike local produce, local processed food is generally more expensive than conventional choices. Think about it this way—how is it possible that you can pay rock-bottom prices for food, like fifty cents for a bag of flour? There are a number of factors that make this possible: meagre wages for workers in countries with non-existent labour laws, child labour, government subsidies, factory farming, and mega corporations running farms. In the Global North, people usually have to pay a minimum wage (though some employers like to get around it whenever possible), which ups the prices significantly. I was paid twelve dollars (Canadian) an hour when I worked at a market farm, and that cost had to be included in the price of the food sold. So think about the impacts of what you're buying beyond the base price. If you have money left over at the end of the month, you have purchasing power. Use it.

It's not possible for everyone to pay that much for food. If you make minimum wage, paying the most basic costs for food and shelter is a struggle. Believe me, I know—I have made the choice between food and rent, and at one point I couldn't fathom spending the money to buy the dirt to plant a small garden to grow our own food. An inability to invest in a future is a big problem when growing food. But if you have the extra money, consider spending it on good food and supporting local, sustainable food systems. I know very wealthy people who penny-pinch at the grocery store and then take several vacations every year (doubly screwing over the planet). If you're buying organic on a budget, there's good news, because food that's local and in season is almost always cheaper than imported organic food.

Another inexpensive way to support local and organic food is—surprise!—to grow your own. Most people don't have outdoor space for a garden, and most landlords don't let renters dig up the garden. Some cool ones do, though, so it never hurts to ask. I've planted a garden at two rentals. If you have a balcony, get some pots out with herbs and maybe some small plants like hot peppers or lettuces. If you have no access to outdoor space at all, the only thing I can really recommend growing indoors for food is herb pots. Herbs are expensive to buy fresh, and things like basil and parsley don't mind growing in a west- or south-facing window, if there's one in your place. And if you are very lucky and have a huge lawn, rip it up! Plant some carrots!

Another great, best, option is a community garden or allotment, which gives you land to grow food in, even if you live in a small apartment. Sometimes they're free or available for a nominal price, depending on your income, and sometimes—often the case in Germany, for example—you have to pay a thousand dollars or more to buy one. It can be hard to get a plot in a community garden, as they're in high demand, but that demand is also driving more to be built. They're popping up more and more in cities these days as people increasingly turn to urban gardening to meet their food needs—something we'll need to embrace in future as climate change continues to disrupt existing food systems.

Organic food isn't a perfect solution. Nothing is. With climate change wreaking havoc on how food can be grown, our consumption of it needs to be more thoughtful than ever. Organic is just one choice in a much larger system—eating local produce, growing your own food, reducing food waste, and more. If organic avocados are five times the price of non-organic ones, likely imported long distances, and wrapped in Styrofoam, do you need to eat one every day?

1   A. Müller et al. (2017); C. Strassner et al. (2015);
    T. Searchinger et al. (2014); D. Tilman and M. Clark (2014).
2   H. Godfray et al. (2018); G. Eshel et al. (2014).
3   M. Barański et al. (2014).
4   USDA (2015).
5   R. Das et al. (2001); H.P. Hutter et al. (2018).
6   E.J. Mrema et al. (2017).
7   R.S. Levine and J. Doull (1992).
8   E.J. Mrema et al. (2017); M. Requena et al. (2019).
9   E.J. Mrema et al. (2017).
10 D. Barndt (2008).
11 R.W. Bretveld et al. (2008).
12 S.M. Holmes (2007).
13 M. Emch (2003).
14 E.J. Mrema et al. (2017); D. Barraza et al. (2011).
15 G. Eshel et al. (2014).

REFERENCES

Barański, M., et al. "Higher Antioxidant and Lower Cadmium Concentrations and Lower Incidence of Pesticide Residues in Organically Grown Crops: A Systematic Literature Review and Meta-Analyses," *British Journal of Nutrition* 112, no. 5 (2014): 794–811.

Barndt, D. *Tangled Routes: Women, Work, and Globalization on the Tomato Trail.* Rowman & Littlefield, 2008.

Barraza, D., et al. "Pesticide Use in Banana and Plantain Production and Risk Perception among Local Actors in Talamanca, Costa Rica," *Environmental Research* 111, no. 5 (2011): 708–17.

Bretveld, R.W., et al. "Reproductive Disorders among Male and Female Greenhouse Workers," *Reproductive Toxicology* 25, no 1 (2008): 107–14.

Das, R., et al. "Pesticide Related Illness among Migrant Farm Workers in the United States," *International Journal of Occupational and Environmental Health* 7, no. 4 (2001): 303–12.

Emch, M. "The Human Ecology of Mayan Cacao Farming in Belize," *Human Ecology* 31, no. 1 (2003): 111–31.

Eshel, G., et al. "Land, Irrigation Water, Greenhouse Gas, and Reactive Nitrogen Burdens of Meat, Eggs, and Dairy Production in the United States," *PNAS* 111, no. 33 (2014).

Godfray, H., et al. "Meat Consumption, Health, and the Environment," *Science* 361, no. 243 (2018).

Holmes, S.M. "'Oaxacans Like to Work Bent Over': The Naturalization of Social Suffering among Berry Farm Workers," *International Migration* 45, no. 3: (2007): 39–68.

Hutter, H.P., et al. "Subjective Symptoms of Male Workers Linked to Occupational Pesticide Exposure on Coffee Plantations in the Jarabacoa Region, Dominican Republic," *International Journal of Environmental Research and Public Health* 15, no. 10 (2018).

Levine, R.S., and J. Doull. "Global Estimates of Acute Pesticide Morbidity and Mortality," *Reviews of Environmental Contamination and Toxicology* 129 (1992): 29–50.

Mrema, E.J., et al. "Pesticide Exposure and Health Problems among Female Horticulture Workers in Tanzania," *Environmental Health Insights* 11 (2017): 1–13.

Müller, A., et al. "Strategies for Feeding the World More Sustainably with Organic Agriculture," *Nature Communications* 8, no. 1290 (2017).

Neff, R.A., et al. "Reducing Meat Consumption in the USA: A Nationally Representative Survey of Attitudes and Behaviours," *Public Health Nutrition* 21, no. 10 (2018): 1835–44.

Requena, M., et al. "Environmental Exposure to Pesticides and Risk of Thyroid Diseases," *Toxicology Letters* 315 (2019): 55–63.

Searchinger, T., et al. *Creating a Sustainable Food Future: A Menu of Solutions to Sustainably Feed More Than 9 Billion People by 2050. World Resources Report 2013–14: Interim Findings.* World Resources Institute, 2014.

Strassner, C., et al. "How the Organic Food System Supports Sustainable Diets and Translates These into Practice," *Frontiers in Nutrition* 2, no. 19 (2015).

Tilman, D., and M. Clark. "Global Diets Link Environmental Sustainability and Human Health," *Nature* 515 (2014): 518–22.

USDA National Organic Program, "Introduction to Organic Practices," *NOP Organic Insider.* (2015).

Acknowledgements

The process of writing this, my first book, in a country where I didn't know anyone or speak the language, in a house that we were renovating ourselves, was one of the most challenging things I've ever done. Thank goodness for video chats and good public transportation in Europe so that I could escape to Hatten any time.

My biggest thank you has to go to Graham, my partner, for supporting me through years of uncertainty as I worked toward a career that I desperately wanted. From working what anthropologist and author David Graeber would definitely categorize as bullshit jobs in Germany to taking the leap to move overseas with me in the first place, you are my steadying hand and greatest love.

Friends both back home in Canada and now in Germany were so supportive through this process—early support from my long-time friends Ashley, Emma, Sarah, and Traci, you gave me the confidence to start along this path in the first place. You are all my favourites. Heidi and Kelly, you get it, and thanks to my friends and colleagues at Baked for offering insights and friendship with other women in this industry. Kris, thank you for getting the ball rolling and for all your help along the way.

After moving, support from newer friends—particularly Kristin and Svenja, who offered so much help for this book, from modelling and testing to providing many of the beautiful ceramics (Zirka Keramik, if you're wondering)—made such a difference.

And my family—thank you to my mom, of course, who first brought me into the kitchen, and my family in Canada. Kristina and Josh, my dad, Aunt Joyce, who taught me so much about gathering, gardening, and preserving, and Pearl for her unwavering kindness and strength. Thank you to my parents for moving to rural Manitoba when I was eight and giving me the opportunity to grow up in a place where I could learn to love Canadian wilderness and, really, an underappreciated province. To my mother-in-law, Colleen, and grandmother-in-law, Ileen, thank you. Ileen (Gran), your cookies are my benchmark.

Then in Germany, Omi, of course, who still doesn't really know what I do for work but is proud anyway. Sonja, Carmen—you both taught me to cook, too—Barbara, the whole Meyer family (Gudrun, du bist die beste), and the Motz-Darrelmanns. Christine, cooking with you made me feel as though I were home, and you improved my German more in a few months than I had in two years. Maria-Anna, you have been my greatest inspiration, a well of understanding, and another aunt.

Lastly, thank you to all of the people who helped me create this book. Bhavna, for your unwavering confidence in this, right from the beginning, and for somehow always knowing exactly what I mean even when I'm not sure. I didn't believe it when you first said we'd become friends during the course of this project (you were right, of course). Rob, for helping me to navigate the parts of this process that pushed the rate of my greying hair to light speed. And Rachel, Lana, Michelle, and everyone else at Appetite and PRHC who, at the time of writing this, I probably haven't talked to yet. There are a shocking number of people involved in the creation of a book, and you are all wonderful and excellent.

This book, over two years of work, wouldn't have been possible without all of you. Thank you.

Index